DATE DUE

JUN 1 5 1994	
MAY 1 0 1996	
APR 0 4 2001	

Economics, Medicine and Health Care

Second Edition

Gavin Mooney

*Director of the Health Economics
Research Unit and Professor of
Health Economics, University
of Aberdeen. Visiting Professor,
Universities of Sydney and Tromsø*

Harvester Wheatsheaf
Barnes & Noble Books

First published 1986
This second edition published 1992 by
Harvester Wheatsheaf,
66 Wood Lane End, Hemel Hempstead,
Hertfordshire, HP2 4RG
A division of
Simon & Schuster International Group

First published in the USA in 1992 by
Barnes & Noble Books
8705 Bollman Place
Savage, Maryland, 20763

Typeset in 10/12 Times by
Mathematical Composition Setters Ltd, Salisbury, Wiltshire, England

Printed and bound in Great Britain by
Billing and Sons Ltd, Worcester

British Library Cataloguing-in-Publication Data

Mooney, Gavin
    Economics, medicine and health care. – 2nd ed.
    I. Title
    362.1

    ISBN 0-7450-1012-1
    ISBN 0-7450-1014-8 pbk

Library of Congress Cataloging-in-Publication Data

Available from the publisher
ISBN 0-389-20991-0

1 2 3 4 5 96 95 94 93 92

List of contents

Contents

List of figures

List of tables

Preface to the first edition

In the process of writing this book I have been keenly aware of my need to learn more and more, particularly about health care. If economists are to succeed in persuading medical, nursing and other health care staff to pay more attention to our discipline, clearly we need to make some effort to understand the difficulties they face in their working environment. I have tried to do so. Certainly, I sympathise with them in the problems of resource allocation with which they have to grapple.

In that respect the book has benefited in being written from the medical campus of the University of Aberdeen, where I have been based since 1974. I would therefore like to express my gratitude to my medical colleagues, in particular Elizabeth Russell and Roy Weir, for their assistance and advice over the last few years.

A number of aspects of the book have benefited from discussions with fellow health economists outside of Aberdeen. In particular, for their assistance and advice, I would like to thank Anita Alban, Yvonne Bally, Tony Culyer, Mike Drummond, Steve Engleman and Alan Williams.

It is, however, my long suffering colleagues in the Health Economics Research Unit who deserve much of my gratitude. In particular, for their comments on various aspects of the book, I would like to thank Anne Ludbrook and Ali McGuire. Rochelle Coutts and Isabel Tudhope coped quite magnificently − as ever − with my handwriting in preparing the typescript, and I am grateful to them. In addition, I wish to thank an anonymous assessor for some very helpful suggestions.

I would also like to thank the many health service staff who have undertaken our correspondence courses in health economics. Some of the material has been drawn from that source and consequently benefited from their comments.

Finally, tak til Anita, Rikke og Johannes.

University of Aberdeen   Gavin Mooney
Aberdeen

Preface to second edition

In revising this book I have been surprised at how much of what was originally written in 1984 and 1985 has survived reasonably intact. Of course things have changed and we have most recently seen the reforms of the NHS coming into place. We have also seen much more attention paid to Quality Adjusted Life Years (QALYs) than was the case in the mid-eighties. But there is a remarkable similarity in terms of the problems that health services still face.

Perhaps it is unrealistic to think that over just a few years there could be radical change. Yet, having been around health care for nearly twenty years, it is rather depressing to see how little does change. I remain convinced of the merits of trying to use economics to assist in the planning, financing and delivery of health care and I believe there is a growing army of health service staff who are increasingly sharing that view. But there is no revolution. It is a gradual and slow process to get any change through. There is a conservatism to health services which is difficult to break through. Indeed one of the clearest advantages of the NHS reforms is that they have been more successful in changing attitudes than any other change in recent years. Whether many of the good aspects of the reforms could have been achieved without quite so much of an upheaval remains a moot point. But the upheaval may have been necessary to get any sort of real change at all.

Beyond the acknowledgements in the preface to the first edition, I now want to add the names of those with whom my thought processes have developed over the last few years. They are many but in particular I would want to recognise Anita Alban, Tony Culyer,

Cam Donaldson, Jack Dowie, Mike Drummond, Ulrika Enemark, Karen Gerard, Matti Hakama, Jane Hall, Uffe Juul Jensen, Ivar Sønbø Kristiansen, Ali McGuire, Jan Abel Olsen and Alan Williams. Additionally, my thanks to two anonymous assessors who have helped me to clarify what I have been trying to say. I would also want to thank my wife Anita, and Rikke and Johannes, yet again for tolerating my absences and even more so my presences.

Farum, Denmark
June 1991   Gavin Mooney

To faither

1

Introduction

From the standpoint of economics there is at least an appearance that much is wrong with health care. Drawing attention to these issues, while an important part of this book, is not its intent. Rather, the purpose is to provide the medical profession and other health care staff with some insights, from the perspective of the discipline of economics, into some of the issues currently facing many health services. It is hoped that such knowledge may help them to pursue better, more efficient and fairer delivery of health care.

It is a commonplace to say that the medical profession is held in a position of trust in society; it is equally a commonplace to state that the individual practitioner is held in a position of trust by the individual patient. A third relevant commonplace is to state that resources generally, and more specifically for health care, are scarce, with the consequence that not all wants or needs for health care can be met. What is not a commonplace − but ought to become one − is the fact that continued lack of general acceptance of the third point and the implications that flow from this lack may lead to an undermining of the trust in the first two with potentially serious consequences not only for the medical profession but for health care generally, and hence health. How do doctors make their decisions? What influences their behaviour? Research to answer these questions is growing but remains thin on the ground. What we do know, however, is that there are very substantial variations in medical practice which appear to imply that doctors are doing very different things when faced with similar patients.[1]

It is relatively easy to be critical of doctors because of their apparent inefficiency. To understand better *why* they are inefficient is both more difficult and more important. Consequently, this book attempts not only to diagnose some of the ills of health care, some of which are indeed iatrogenic, but also to suggest some appropriate (i.e. the most cost-effective) treatments.

Our starting text is simply, 'In the beginning, middle and end was, is and will be scarcity of resources.' This is the essence of economics but unfortunately not, at least not sufficiently, of the science of medicine. It is around the concept of scarcity that this book revolves.

In the next chapter there is a brief introduction to economics and health economics which in no way does justice to the discipline but will provide a guide at minimum cost to doctors and others who have previously not encountered economics (at least not as a discipline — doctors inevitably encounter economics every day, even if they sometimes fail to appreciate the fact). How markets operate and the techniques of economic appraisal are also discussed in Chapter 2.

The third chapter considers a fundamental aspect of the whole debate about health care; that is, health care as a 'commodity' (in the sense that like cars, cakes and candelabra, it provides benefit, satisfaction, utility to consumers). But it is a commodity which in some respects at least is rather different from many, indeed most, other goods and services.

In the fourth chapter the issue of quantifying health is outlined and the need for developing health status indices discussed. The use of 'QALYs' (Quality Adjusted Life Years) is highlighted. This is followed in Chapter 5 by a debate on whose values are relevant in health care, together with consideration of how economists have tackled the problem of valuing human life. Given that this is a task which is anathema to many health care professionals, it is important to ascertain why it cannot and should not be avoided.

This debate is continued in Chapter 6, where the concepts of demand and of need for health care are examined. This discussion is then set against the background of the so-called 'agency relationship', a concept very familiar to and scarcely novel for doctors but only relatively recently discovered by economists. Here the various strands — scarcity, the nature of health care as an economic good and values in health care — are brought together. Not that in this chapter any resolution of the tensions between these different facets and the actors playing the different roles is offered. (This is dealt with in the concluding chapter.)

Chapter 7 turns to some aspects of medical ethics, not only to make many readers feel more comfortable on more familiar territory but also to raise some slightly different questions both about and arising from medical ethics than is perhaps normally the case when such topics are debated. That then allows an indication of the current conflict that apparently exists between economics and medicine. In reality the conflict is more between, on the one hand, a rational acceptance of and approach to the issue of scarcity and, on the other, medical ethics (partly in principle but more so in practice). Indeed, in many ways it is the nature, source, problems and resolution of this conflict that are the central themes of this book.

Chapter 8 is about equity and the difficulties of defining it in practice. The link between ethics and equity is highlighted.

In Chapter 9 a relatively novel way of looking at the way in which different societies organise and finance their health care system is presented. Within this setting the rationale for different systems is discussed from the community's point of view. Essentially the arguments here are ideological, but there is discussion of an interesting (and defensible) rationale to support different ideologies.

What emerges from this is that the medical profession has attempted to retain, certainly individually but perhaps also collectively, an ideology or at least *modus operandi* which is more appropriate in a market-orientated health care system. Indeed, it is suggested in Chapter 10 that in NHS-type systems medical doctors may have usurped some of the benefit of such systems not motivated by financial gain per se but rather as a means of defending their status. In this context the opportunity is taken to examine the reforms of the NHS. The concluding chapter also points to a solution to some of the problems raised earlier in this book. The solution – essentially attempting to ensure that the objectives of the community *qua* community and those of the medical profession, both individually and collectively, become the same through the introduction of a new health care ethical code – is a simple one, at least in principle. Some mechanisms for providing the incentives for the medical profession to equate their objectives with the community's (or at least to behave as if this were the case) are presented.

It is further emphasised that these mechanisms are wholly commensurate with, and may even enhance, most medical ethics including the much-abused clinical freedom, provided medical ethics remains in its legitimate territory. Such demonstration should prevent besieged medical readers from labelling the process as unreasonable, unethical or impractical.

Notes

1. R. G. Evans, 'The dog in the night-time: medical practice variations of health policy' in *The Challenges of Medical Practice Variations*, eds T.F. Andersen and G.H. Mooney (Macmillan: London, 1990).

2

Economics and health economics

The social science – not a 'gay science' ... which finds the secret of this Universe in 'supply and demand' ... what we might call ... the dismal science.

(Thomas Carlyle, 'On the Nigger Question' (1849))

2.1   Resource allocation problems

Economics has been defined by Samuelson[1] as 'the study of how men and society end up choosing, with or without the use of money, to employ scarce productive resources that could have alternative uses, to produce various commodities and distribute them for consumption, now or in the future, among various people and groups in society. It analyses the costs and benefits of improving patterns of resource allocation.'

Within this statement, which encompasses much more than many readers might have imagined, there are a number of important issues. In this chapter, rather briefly, I want to point out some of the main ones and exemplify them, where possible, in terms of health care or everyday life.

It would, however, be potentially misleading to venture into the process without first explaining that economics is a discipline, a recognised body of thought and not just a bag of tools. *Health economics* is the discipline of economics applied to the *topic* of health. (See Williams for a more detailed discussion of this issue.[2])

5

Consequently, what health economists are doing when attempting to educate others − be they doctors, nurses, administrators, politicians, patients or the public generally − is primarily to try to change a way of thinking. It is not that economists would claim that their way of thinking is always 'superior'. It is unlikely to be the most helpful discipline in trying to solve a problem of nuclear physics or to reduce one's golf handicap. Yet there are economic questions surrounding these issues. How important is it to solve these problems? What proportion of society's *scarce* resources should be devoted to them? Why is it that as an individual I may devote more of my resources to the second (apparently trivial) problem than to the first? What is the most cost-effective solution to getting my handicap down − new clubs, lessons or practice? Or maybe I would be better giving up golf and taking up tennis or tiddly-winks instead?

There *are* economic issues here. They may well not be dominant ones but there are few areas of life where economics does not come into play in some way or other. It seems difficult to believe, but is nonetheless true, that economists have to try to persuade anyone that economics is important in health care − with some nations devoting 10 per cent of their total resources to health care (and considerably more to health), with technological advances appearing or developing much more rapidly than the ability and willingness to pay for them, with debates about the economic organisation of health care, questions about the role of prices and remuneration of manpower (e.g. doctors), and so on.

Thus, the issues of choice, as spelt out in Samuelson's definition, are relevant in health care. How much of society's scarce resources should be devoted to health, to health care? What priority should be given to the elderly *vis-à-vis* the mentally ill? What does 'giving priority' mean? Should more surgical patients be treated as day patients? When and where should that new hospital be built? Is prevention 'better' than cure, and if so, for which diseases/ conditions? What are the implications for the health service, for the community and for individual patients of introducing or increasing fees for consultation with general practitioners? What happens when we raise prescription charges?

Some of these questions appear more 'overtly' economic than others: for example, when, as with the last two, the question of money prices arises. But in fact all of them involve choice about the use of scarce resources.

At this point, lest the reader begin to believe that he has already learned enough about the arrogance of economics, it is worth stressing that it is not suggested that economics alone can answer these questions. Indeed economics will not even be the dominant discipline in trying to do so. There are essentially two points being made: (1) the occasions on which economics, particularly as a way of thinking, is likely to prove helpful are more frequent than most non-economists might expect; and (2) partly because of this but also because of the methodological underpinning of all economics, an injection of such a way of thinking is likely to provide new and important insights which might otherwise have been overlooked.

Economics exists as a science of human behaviour for two simple reasons. First, there is a finite limit to the resources available to mankind as a whole, to any individual society, any organisation or, indeed, any individual. Second, as individuals and societies, it appears that to all intents and purposes our wants are insatiable. These two factors taken together mean that choice has to be exercised not only about what to do but also (and equally important) what to leave undone.

It follows from this that the concept of opportunity cost (which is rather different from the concept of cost which most non-economists understand) is central to economics. Opportunity cost entails sacrifice. Given that resources are scarce if we decide to use them in one particular way, there is an opportunity forgone to obtain the benefits of using these resources in some other way. If I devote time (a scarce resource) to practising golf to lower my golf handicap, there is an opportunity cost involved in that I cannot use that same time to watch football, go to a concert or write books. If another CT scanner is bought, the costs and use represent forgone opportunities to provide benefits, from more geriatric beds, more health visiting or, in the end, more golf lessons or other forms of non-health care personal spending. Dr Paul *always* robs Dr, Mr or Master Peter. As we shall see later, it is the *attempt* – inevitably forlorn – to ignore, by-pass or overcome this basic law of economics which leads to frustration and inefficiency in the health care sector.

This concept of 'opportunity cost' encourages us to place

monetary values on 'costs' which might not normally be seen as having pound signs in front of them, or indeed as costs at all. Thus, in the example of the use of time for practising golf, the opportunity cost may be in measurable income forgone in not working. If this is the next best use of my time, then the amount of income forgone is a measure of the benefit I perceive I get from practising golf. (The perception issue is important: if my golf handicap does not come down then I may realise that I would have been better off in writing than practising. Nonetheless, I made the decision on the basis of my perception of the opportunity costs *at the time* I made the decision.)

Thus, in our private lives, albeit not necessarily wholly consciously, we attempt to maximise benefit from whatever resources we have at our disposal. This is essentially what efficiency is: getting the most out of the resources available. For example, some readers may have a penchant for avocado pears, as I do. For others their tastes may be different: they may prefer oranges. Nonetheless, there is a limit to the number of avocado pears that I can or want to consume. At *some* stage, as I go on buying more and more avocado pears in a particular week, I will decide that I would rather have an orange than yet another avocado pear. Indeed, over a year it is likely that out of my budget for fruit I consume a hundred avocado pears and fifty oranges.

Now, before the reader gains the impression that I spend an inordinate amount of time in fruit shops trying to decide how to deploy my fruit budget, it has to be emphasised that this is a *model* of how I behave. Given certain fixed prices for these goods, I perceive myself to be better off with this mix than if say the numbers above were in reverse order. Or again, assuming for simplicity that the prices of the two fruits are the same, then what emerges from my behaviour is that I would rather have this mix than, say, ninety-nine avocado pears and fifty-one oranges, because the loss of the hundredth avocado pear is not compensated for by the gain of the fifty-first orange.

A point of importance in this is that the question of decision-making is 'at the margin'; that is, around the question of the hundredth avocado pear and the fiftieth orange. It is here that priorities are really sorted out. Thus, to prefer (or have higher priority for) avocado pears to oranges does not mean that I will always be buying avocado pears and oranges. Nor indeed does it mean going on until the last one bought yields no benefit, because there is an opportunity cost in terms of forgone oranges. Thus, priorities are not absolute or 'lexicographic'; that is, we do not order our expenditure in such a way that we take care of our *total* want for our top priority, then move to our second priority, and so on. We adjust our consumption to try to make sure that we maximise benefit; we buy a little less of this and a little more of something else.

But what if suddenly the price of avacado pears doubles? Now fewer avocados but more oranges will be bought because the opportunity cost of avocado pears (in terms of forgone oranges) has risen. Thus, the determination of the optimal use of my fruit budget is a function not only of my liking for oranges and avocados but the relative costs of these products to me (in this, case, money prices).

What the above discussion shows is that:

1. Priorities are not absolute nor follow a lexicographic ordering.
2. They are a function of both benefits and costs.
3. The important area for decision-making is at the margin.
4. The assessment of both costs and benefits is subjective.
5. Different individuals may perceive costs and benefits (of the same things) differently.

In the context of health care, examples of these economic messages are, in turn, as follows:

1. 'Priority for the elderly' does not mean devoting all expenditure or indeed all of any increased expenditure to the elderly, nor that we should fulfil the needs of the elderly *in toto* before considering other uses of resources.
2. In deciding what and how much to do for the elderly, we should consider not only the benefits any action will provide but the costs (the opportunity costs) of forgoing benefits for the mentally ill, pregnant women, and so on.
3. What priority setting means in practice is deciding whether we should spend an extra £1 million on the elderly, the mentally ill or pregnant women and then perhaps deciding if we should spend another £1 million on the elderly, and so on.
4. There are no 'scientifically' objective measures of the benefits or costs of helping the elderly or any other client or patient group.

5. Your perception of these costs and benefits may be quite
    different from mine.

2.2   Supply and demand: the market

Health care markets seem to operate rather differently from other
markets. Nonetheless it is important that readers have some understanding of how a basic market operates. It is not the intention to
suggest that this model is appropriate to health care. Indeed it will
be argued later that markets for health care tend to fail for various
reasons.

From the fact that resources are scarce and man's wants seemingly insatiable emerge the important notions in economics of
'demand' and 'supply'. Demand is about how willing consumers
are to pay for different goods and services. Supply is about the
production side and how costs of factors of production and prices
of the final product affect the amount of goods supplied. These
ideas are relevant to health care, although not necessarily in the
unbridled and sometimes rather naive form presented in this section. However, grasping the concepts presented here at least allows
the reader to get hold of the basics of *economics*; we can worry
more about the application to health care later.

As consumers we have various 'wants' for goods and services
which we desire (i.e. which would give us some positive satisfaction). Combining 'wants' with limited income, we have the
notion of (consumer) demand or willingness to pay.

Demand assumes that the best people to decide on the values to
be attached to various goods and commodities are normally those
who will benefit from them (i.e. the consumers). It assumes it is
they who are the most knowledgeable and best placed to make the
appropriate value judgments. It is from this notion that the important principle of 'consumer sovereignty' emerges, the idea that
consumers should be sovereign on the demand side of the market-
place. (Later, in Chapter 3, we will discuss the problems which arise
when consumers are not very knowledgeable about the relevant
commodities, as for example in health care.)

The demand curve for a good or service shows the relationship
between its price and the quantity wished to be purchased (when
income, tastes and the prices of all other goods and services are

held constant). The nature of demand is such that it will normally be the case that the demand curve will slope downwards from left to right — indicating that the lower the price, the greater the quantity demanded (see Figure 2.1).

Lying behind demand is the concept of 'utility', which is economists' jargon for satisfaction. Economists assume that the greater the utility obtained from a visit to the cinema, the greater will be the price that anyone will be prepared to pay for it. The way that individuals deploy their incomes across the very wide range of goods and services available indicates some attempt to 'maximise utility'.

If all goods were offered at the same price, it would be rational for the individual to consume those goods which had the greatest utility attached to them. However, this would not necessarily mean consuming one of each of such goods because more utility might be obtained from the consumption of say two oranges and one apple than from one orange, one apple and one pear.

It is at this point that the concept of 'marginal utility' comes into play and, in particular, that of 'diminishing marginal utility'. Thus, if I consume two oranges a day, my utility will be greater than if I consume only one. But it is unlikely that I will obtain twice as much utility. Thus, if we say that 'marginal utility' is the additional

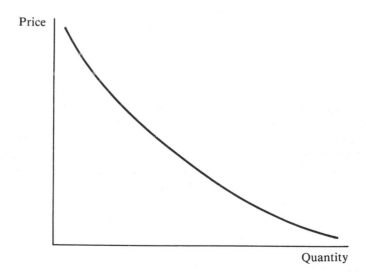

Figure 2.1 Downward sloping demand curve

utility from consuming one extra unit of a good, then diminishing marginal utility means simply that as more and more of a particular good is consumed, the utility obtained from each additional unit of consumption will tend to fall.

To maximise my utility, what I want to ensure is that the last pence spent on each good yields the same utility to me. If this is not the case and I get more utility from the last pence I spend on carrots than from the last pence spent on sprouts, then I can increase my overall utility by spending more on carrots and less on sprouts. It has to be emphasised that this is a theory. It is not intended to be a description of consumers' thinking when they go out shopping. It is the 'as if' principle; that is, consumers behave 'as if' they were thinking along these lines.

While different objectives can be specified for producers of goods and services, economists frequently assume that producers attempt to maximise profits – the difference between what they receive from selling their goods (revenue) and what it costs the producer to make the goods (production costs). The higher prices are, *ceteris paribus*, the more profit the supplier of the goods will make. The prices of other goods can affect the supply of a particular good. This is because if other prices rise while the price of the good in which we have a particular interest remains steady, it becomes relatively less attractive to producers to supply this particular good.

Technology also has an influence on the supply of goods and services. For example, the technological 'revolution' that has taken place in the production of computers has had a considerable influence on supply through reducing the cost of producing them.

Thus, the supply of a good or service is a function of the price of that good or service, the objectives of those producing the good or service, the prices of other goods and services, the prices of factors of production and the technology involved in the production processes.

The supply curve shows the relationship between price and quantity supplied, when everything else (e.g. the price of other goods) is held constant.

But why should the supply curve slope upwards from left to right? It is simply a question of incentives for the producer. The higher the price of a particular good, the more resources will the producer be prepared to devote to producing that good. Therefore, if the price of apples rises, and nothing else changes, the producer of apples can increase his profits by putting more resources into the production of apples and fewer into, say, the production of pears. He might also convert some of his orchard from pear trees to apple trees if he believes that the new price is likely to be sustained.

Just as utility lies behind the concept of 'demand', so cost lies behind the concept of 'supply'. A firm will only supply goods of a particular type if it can at least cover its costs. This is why there is a basic relationship between price and quantity supplied. The higher the price, the more costs are likely to be met and the greater the profits to be obtained. Supply and demand can now be brought together in the context of market prices, as in Table 2.1 for potatoes.

Now in the first situation, (i), the price per ton of potatoes is £100. At this price the quantity demanded per month is 500 tons and the quantity supplied per month is only 180 tons. Thus, there is 'excess demand'. Similarly in situation (ii) there is an 'excess demand' of 160 tons (400 tons minus 240 tons). In both situations there will be frustrated potential purchasers, at least some of whom will be prepared to bid-up prices in an attempt to obtain more potatoes. Further, producers will be aware that they could raise their prices and still sell all their potatoes. There is thus pressure from both consumers and producers to raise the price of potatoes.

In situations (iv), (v) and (vi) there is 'excess supply'. Producers will be faced with unsold potatoes unless they lower their prices, and consumers, becoming aware that the market is flooded with potatoes, will be less prepared to pay high prices for potatoes. There is thus pressure from both consumers and producers to reduce the price of potatoes.

Table 2.1 Six situations in the market for potatoes

Situation	Price of potatoes per ton (£s)	Quantity demanded per month (tons)	Quantity supplied per month (tons)	Excess demand (+) excess supply (−) (tons)
(i)	100	500	180	+320
(ii)	150	400	240	+160
(iii)	200	320	320	0
(iv)	250	260	400	−140
(v)	300	220	500	−280
(vi)	350	200	620	−420

When demand is greater than supply there will be pressure to increase price; when supply is greater than demand there will be pressure to reduce price. When there is neither excess demand nor excess supply (i.e. the market is in equilibrium) there will be no pressure to increase or decrease price. In the table above the equilibrium price is £200 per ton.

2.3   Economic appraisal

This section formulates a little more rigorously what has been said about evaluation and priority setting. As Samuelson's last sentence in his definition of economics indicates, economists are much concerned with the weighing-up of costs and benefits in health care and elsewhere. Certainly it would be wrong to suggest that health economics equals cost-benefit analysis of health and health care. Yet of all the techniques of economic analysis available to the practitioner in the system, economic appraisal is perhaps the most relevant. The cost-benefit approach (or 'economic appraisal' as it is sometimes called) is already fairly well known in health care circles. This is not surprising. For can anyone deny the essential truths of cost-benefit analysis – that we should only do those things where benefits exceed costs, that the judgment as to what constitutes costs and benefits should be made on the broadest of social canvasses, and that the valuation of benefits and costs is normally best made by those who are advantaged and disadvantaged by their existence?

Despite these truths, it remains the case that the understanding of the principles of the cost-benefit approach remains poor in health care. The practice is rather infrequent and often of low quality. Here I want to spell out briefly what the principles are. (For more detail, see Drummond[3] and Ludbrook[4].) Why there are problems in practice will become apparent as the book proceeds. The problems will be addressed explicitly in the final chapter together with some suggestions on how they can be overcome.

The cost-benefit approach deals with two concepts of efficiency, and here we need a little jargon: 'X-efficiency' and 'allocative efficiency'. The former accepts a particular objective as given and is then concerned only with how to meet this objective at least cost. The technique used to address this question of 'how' is cost-effectiveness analysis (CEA).

Allocative efficiency is addressed by the technique of cost benefit analysis (CBA), which considers how to maximise the benefit from available resources. In this case, objectives are not predetermined, and each objective has to fight with all others to be implemented. Thus, CBA deals with the question of 'whether'. In the form of what has been called 'marginal analysis' – with issues 'at the margin' of programmes – CBA also helps in considering the question of 'how much'. CBA is performed on a wide canvas. *All* costs and benefits arising as a result of implementing a particular project, no matter on whom they fall, are relevant. This is because in health care we are concerned with the welfare of society at large and not simply the health service. Thus, economists would argue that it is too narrow to consider increased community care purely in terms of the health effects on the clients and the costs to the health service since there are likely to be implications for other social services (e.g. local authority social work departments) for the clients in other than health effects (e.g. cost of living in the community) and indeed for clients' relatives (e.g. a son or daughter doing some of the caring in the community). The viewpoint is thus a societal one.

With CEA it will normally be the case that the costs will be more narrowly defined, often purely in terms of those falling on the health service budget. In practice however, a wider view of costs is often taken, similar to that adopted in CBA.

Since CBA attempts to help to decide if something should be done, there are two important principles on which it is founded:

1. Only do those things where benefits exceed costs.
2. Do not do those things where costs exceed benefits.

It follows that since costs are often measured in money terms, to make them commensurate, economists also want to measure benefits in money terms. Clearly, CEA, which requires only some physical and not monetary measure of output or effectiveness, has the advantage over CBA of not getting into the difficult emotive realms of benefit valuation. But it is more restrictive in the questions it can address, particularly as in practice it has difficulty in coping with more than one output. (This is because once there is more than one output, assuming they do not always vary directly with each other, then relative weights have to be attached to these different outputs.)

In these circumstances another form of analysis comes into play – cost-utility analysis (CUA). This uses a multi-dimensional measure of health, usually called the 'QALY' or Quality Adjusted Life Year, on the output side. This attempts to combine quantity of life with quality of life in a single index. Clearly insofar as it can succeed in achieving this, then there are great advantages over the single-dimensional output that cost-effectiveness studies can deal with. More detailed discussion of QALYs per se follows in Chapter 4.

CUA also allows under certain restrictive assumptions a way of approaching allocative efficiency, essentially which programmes, the elderly, the mentally ill, etc., should get priority, but which avoids the necessity of going as far as CBA and the problems in that form of analysis which arise from the need to value the outputs in money terms. Indeed it is at least partly because of these advantages that CUA has become rather popular in the last few years.

But there are problems. Those specifically related to QALYs will be discussed in Chapter 4. Here briefly I would simply mention some of the problems of CUA even if QALYs are taken to be an acceptable measure of health.

CUA assumes that there are no other objectives to health care than health maximisation. Yet there may be other aspects that people care about, e.g. information, and which QALYs would not cover.

There are usually equity objectives in health care and it is far from clear that CUAs handle these issues well (an aspect we will return to in Chapter 9 which deals specifically with equity). However for a contrary view see Culyer.[5]

CUA tends to be restricted to health service resources on the cost side. Indeed it can be argued that it has to be. This is because if we are saying that the goal of health services is to maximise health then clearly within the health service budget, if health can be bought more cheaply with programme A than programme B, then we should first invest in programme A. The opportunity cost is wholly in terms of health. But if we allow other costs to be included, such as those falling on patients, then the opportunity cost of, for example, patient time may be in all sorts of things and not just health.

To be clear on these points: CUA, assuming QALYs adequately measure health, can be used to promote allocative efficiency provided that we are not concerned with equity; provided that the output of health services is purely health and nothing else; and provided that we are only interested in the efficiency with which health service resources are used and not the resources, such as those of patients, outside the health service. This is not to be overcritical of CUA but simply to put it in perspective in terms of some of the restrictions on its use. It should be noted too that these restrictions apply primarily to its use in the context of allocative efficiency. For more discussion of some of these issues see Mooney and Olsen.[6]

In marginal analysis the same basic rules apply as in cost-benefit, except that they are now applied 'at the margin'. If no budget constraint exists, then a programme should be expanded or contracted to the point where marginal benefit equals marginal cost; if there is a budget constraint, then all programmes should operate at a level whereby the ratio of marginal benefit to marginal cost is the same for all. (This 'law' is the same as saying that the last pound spent on each programme should yield the same benefit and is the equivalent of message 3 spelt out in section 2.1.)

When costs and benefits occur in time matters. For example, even in an inflationless world faced with paying, say, £220 for a television set now or being able to have the set but delaying the payment for one year, I would prefer the latter. I still get the benefit of the set from now but the cost to me is less because I can invest, say, £200 *now* and with interest have £220 available in a year's time. In other words, the *present* value of the cost is £200, not £220.

Let's say that if I had to pay £220 now, I would not buy the set; if £200 now, I would buy it. The fact that the present value of the cost is £200 and not £220 makes the difference between buying and not buying. In other words, I weigh up the present value of the stream of benefits (pleasure) I expect to get from the set against the present value of the costs, and if the former exceeds the latter, I buy; if not, I don't.

This process works equally well on the benefit side but, in a sense, in reverse. Benefits in the future are valued at less than benefits in the present. Perhaps here we need to recognise that in addition to the investment argument (which is simply another facet of the concept of opportunity cost), as individuals we have a preference for 'good' things now rather than later (and the reverse with 'bad' things). This may be because of a simple time-preference (psychologically), but in addition there are the factors of uncertainty (e.g. we might die or have changed tastes in the future) and the idea of 'diminishing marginal utility of income'. This slightly awesome expression simply means that an extra £100 is likely to have a higher value if our current income is £500 than if it is £50,000. Assuming that our real incomes will increase through time, then this is another argument for 'discounting' the future.

This process of discounting is particularly important where the *timing* of costs and benefit is very different. For example, in preventive programmes (such as many screening services) there may be a gap of several years between when the major costs are incurred and when the benefits will arise. Because of the need to discount, this will have the effect of reducing the present value of the benefits much more than that of the costs. (It might be argued that this explains why anti-smoking campaigns for young people have tried to move away from emphasising the long-term benefits of mortality reduction to more short-term benefits such as smokers not being as appealing to the opposite sex.)

Both costs and benefits are subjective concepts. It is frequently possible to assume that the costs of, say, nursing time are represented fairly accurately by the wages and overheads associated with the employment of nurses. Other costs may be very difficult or even impossible to value (e.g. the time spent by a son or daughter in looking after an ageing parent). However, even when values cannot be assigned, at least noting these intangible costs means that they are less likely to be lost sight of in any decision taken.

On the benefit side there are problems in measuring and valuing health (an issue covered in greater detail in Chapters 4 and 5). But the essence of the value question here is that it cannot be avoided. Any decision to spend £1 million on saving a life means that the life is being valued at at least £1 million; a decision *not* to proceed implies a value of less than £1 million.

Related to the issue of how to value is that of who should do the valuing. Returning to my golf practice and my purchase of avocado pears, decisions about time and expenditure of resources devoted to them are probably best left to me. (Who knows better than I do the benefits of these activities to me and the opportunity costs involved for me?) This is known as 'consumer sovereignty', a concept dear to the hearts of many economists. But in health care, particularly in a national health service, is the 'consumer' best placed to decide on his or her consumption of health care? Certainly most of us may be prepared to accept on occasions that 'the doctor knows best'. Does this mean that doctors' sovereignty should apply in health care? Perhaps − but bear in mind that at least part of the reason why health care is generally not available in an unregulated market-place is born of the view that we ought not to leave decision-making in this important area of life to doctors, patients or some combination of these parties. Should we then have politicians' sovereignty in health care?

Answers to these questions are central to the debate about the nature, organisation and financing of health care. Given that, they are clearly also important to the theme of this book. Consequently, these questions are addressed in more detail in later chapters.

2.4   Conclusions

Economics is about choice; it is about opportunity cost; it is about maximising the benefit to society from the resources available.

The goal is efficiency − getting the most we can out of the available labour, land and capital, often tempered by some concern with equity. The viewpoint is society's at large and not any single individual or individual group's perspective. The ethic is that of the common good and, indeed, not settling for doing good but doing better, more fairly.

It is therefore unfortunate that economics has been dubbed the dismal science. More accurately, it is the joyful art since it attempts to maximise social benefit from the resources available subject to reasonable concerns with justice. It is thus the task of economists to 'spread a little happiness' or, more accurately, to spread as much happiness as resources will permit − a laudable goal indeed. Fascinating then that in health care, where caring and humanitarian instincts pervade discussion and action, there is a reluctance to embrace this joyful art. Is economics getting it wrong? Is health care not about efficiency (i.e. about delivering the best/most health possible)? Are doctors not the caring people we all believe them to be? Or do they care about something else?

Of key significance to efficiency in any economic system is the knowledge required by the actors. Indeed, good information is the basis of the freedom that proponents of market economics suggest is one of its greatest virtues. Yet in health care there has to be concern about the extent and distribution of knowledge, and consequently the success in pursuing efficiency and in turn the nature and protection of freedom. Jennett,[7] formerly Dean of the Medical Faculty in Glasgow and a leading expert in technology assessment, in discussing some of the vexed issues involved in creating a more rational health care system, refers to an analogy drawn by Hiatt[8] with herdsmen grazing on common land: 'Once capacity is approached on the shared pasture, the attempts of individual herdsmen to increase their holdings has little benefit on the general welfare. Eventually, freedom on the common brings ruin to all.' What will be an important focus of this book is the extent to which this parallel with the medical profession can be taken.

These issues are central to this book. We will return to them. In the meantime we need to investigate the nature of health and health care. It is to this that the next chapter is devoted.

Notes

1. P.A. Samuelson, *Economics* (McGraw-Hill: Tokyo, 1976), p. 5.
2. A. Williams, 'One economist's view of social medicine', *Journal of Epidemiology and Community Health*, 33 (1979).
3. M.F. Drummond, *Principles of Economic Appraisal in Health Care* (Oxford Medical Publications: Oxford, 1980).
4. A. Ludbrook, 'Using economic appraisal in health services research', *Health Bulletin*, 48 (1990).
5. A.J. Culyer, 'Inequality of health services is, in general, desirable' in *Acceptable Inequalities*, ed. D.G. Green (IEA: London, 1988).
6. G. Mooney and J.A. Olsen, 'QALYs: where next?' in *Providing Health Care: The Economics of Alternative Systems of Finance and Delivery*, eds A. McGuire, P. Fenn and K. Mayhew (Oxford University Press: Oxford, 1991).
7. B. Jennett, 'The cost of rescue and the price of survival' in *Clinical Practice and Economics*, eds C.I. Philips and J.N. Wolfe (Pitman Medical: Tunbridge Wells, 1977), p 54.
8. H.H. Hiatt, 'Protecting the medical commons: Who is responsible?' *New England Journal of Medicine*, 293 (1975).

3

The nature of the commodity health care

3.1   Introduction

One of the central issues in health care is that of deciding how to value health. Since resources are limited in all health services and the 'need' for health care is dynamic and ever increasing, value judgments are required about priorities. What health service objectives should get higher weight? Should the acute services get more or less resources? Should the elderly get more or less resources? Who should have a transplanted kidney, and who should not? Should all mothers have their babies delivered in hospital (indeed, in a specialist maternity unit)?

This chapter begins a discussion on some of the issues involved in valuation of health – problems associated with health and health care per se, problems of ethics and measurement, problems of demand and consumer sovereignty, problems of measuring health and problems of actually placing values on health outputs such as lives saved. Aspects of these issues are debated further in Chapters 4 to 6.

Economists have been much intrigued in recent years with the nature of the 'commodity' health care, particularly in trying to explain why markets ('non-markets' may be a more appropriate description) for health care differ from those for most other goods. It can be frustrating (at least for economists) to discover that textbook economics does not explain very well the market for health care in terms of conventional supply and demand analysis, as spelt out in the previous chapter. It may seem a little strange that anyone should want to consider health and health care alongside avocado pears, golf clubs and concerts, but this is the way in which economists tend to think. This chapter attempts to show that much of relevance to debates about health care policy can be gleaned by an examination of some of the rather peculiar attributes of health and health care.[1] I will first consider health and then turn to health care.

3.2   Defining health

It is interesting and perhaps significant in terms of the difficulty of the task that we need to begin by asking what health is. Yet we must because it is a concept which is difficult to define and subject to many different interpretations, some of which, but only some, are relevant to our discussion.

The World Health Organisation defines health as 'a state of complete physical, mental and social well-being, and not merely the absence of disease or infirmity'.[2] Such a definition, while one with which it is only too easy to agree, at the same time is one with which it is difficult to operate in practice if we are to attempt to consider the nature of health and later the measurement and valuation of health.

To most medical doctors, fascinatingly, the question of defining health and ill health is of little, if any, relevance to them. As Kosa and Robertson observe: 'The practising physician tends to regard health, illness, disability and death in their concrete relevance ... definitions of health and illness appear to him as matters all too abstract and removed from the current problems.'[3] However, as the same authors continue: 'if a national health policy has to be considered ... the unique clinical observations need to be synthesised into a general conceptual framework where health and illness become social as well as medical phenomena'.

There can be major differences in how health is viewed, and the weight attached to these differing views in different contexts is important. The issue of the individual doctor's perception and the broader community perspective is first raised here. It is an issue that will plague us all the way through this book, just as it plagues all debates about health care policy. It is central to the issue of medical ethics and its conflict with rational resource allocation. Yet it is an issue that the medical profession individually and collectively tend to ignore or seek to avoid.

Health can be viewed in several different ways. For example, Twaddle suggests that from a biological standpoint 'perfect health' might be seen as 'a state in which every cell of the body is functioning at optimum capacity and in perfect harmony with each other cell'.[4] Again from a social standpoint, 'perfect health may be a state in which an individual's capacities for taste and role performance are optimised'.

The concepts of health and sickness can be very different depending upon the definition used and particularly the standpoint adopted. Thus, 'there is a wide consensus among medical people that illness is any state that has been diagnosed as such by a competent professional ... Alternatively, there is a view that whoever feels ill should be regarded as sick.'[5] These different definitions and the different standpoints from which they emerge are of much importance in considering the nature of health and later health care as a commodity.

3.3 Health and health care

We can circumvent *some* of the problems here by suggesting that the real interest of this book and what is central to our debate is the demand and supply of health care rather than health per se. But we need to be careful lest the impression be given that the two can be seen as wholly separate.

First, there seems little value in health per se. Rather its value stems from its possession allowing us to act out more fulfilling lives in terms of work and play than we might otherwise do. This immediately leads to various complications in that to be interested in the concept of health means to be interested in all aspects of life from which individuals derive satisfaction, since in extreme ill-health all of these may be snuffed out. Add in the fact that ill-health itself comes in many guises – pain, physical disability, mental impairment, and so on, each with differing degrees of severity – and the problems grow, becoming infinitely greater once we accept that a nominally equal state of ill-health may have very different implications for different individuals. The loss of a leg or an arm would clearly create considerably greater problems for a professional footballer or a classical pianist respectively, than for a health economist. Thus, the demand for health is largely a derived demand, derived from the value we place on being fit and well to lead fulfilling lives.

Second, while health (however defined) is supplied by health care systems, it is also supplied through many other agencies. Indeed, it might be argued that the main supplier of health for any individual is the individual him or herself through sensible diet, jogging, and so on. Health is also supplied through prevention of road accidents, clean air regulations, occupational health and safety regulations and building regulations. We ought not to lose sight of this fact.

Third, there is a definite if often ill-specified relationship between health and health care. While we can promote our own health in many ways, for most of us it is difficult to envisage any other reason for approaching the health care system than for reasons of health promotion. There is a sense in which any demand we have for health care is derived from our demand for health; that is, we are prepared to lie in a hospital bed not because we enjoy it per se but because we hope that by doing so we will attain a higher level of health. The demand for health care is thus also a derived demand, derived from our demand for health insofar as the health care system can, as we see it, promote that health.

Related to these broad issues of the demand for health and the demand for health care, one economist, Grossman, has suggested that the way that we view health ought to be as a durable capital asset which is a fundamental commodity underlying many others.[6] This approach is based on the notion that health is produced by households, each household having a demand for health which may or may not on occasion become a demand for health care.

In this way, households have demands for many goods which may not necessarily or always be desired solely for their own sake. For example, food, housing and physical exercise are demanded at least in part for their health-producing attributes. This idea of seeing the demand (willingness to pay) for goods as the demand for the different attributes of the good can be useful in a number of instances. Thus, while many smokers do realise that smoking is bad for their health (there is some negative utility in the sense that they would be willing to pay to *remove* this attribute), this is more than compensated for by the positive utility from the other attributes of smoking. (If we make cigarettes 'safer', almost certainly the number of cigarettes smoked will increase, not because smokers are perverse but simply because the demand for a safe product is likely to be greater than the demand for a risky one, *ceteris paribus*. This may be a partial explanation for what happened when filter cigarettes came on the market.)

Thus, in this view the focus is on the household with the formal health care sector only coming into play when the household demands it as part of its demand for health. This is a potentially useful way of considering health and points perhaps to the need for the formal health care services to do more to promote awareness of the health producing activities which go on outside the health care sector. (More tangibly it might be argued that what the job of health educationalists or prevention officers in health care should be is to mobilise resources for health from *outside* the formal health care sector. This happens already – see the *Report of the Royal Commission on the NHS* on the question of seat-belt wearing in the United Kingdom[7] – but this whole idea of the 'demand for health' suggests that much more might be done.)

But there are dangers in the approach. Certainly let's try to persuade people to eat apples if it is healthy to do so, but it is important to appreciate at the same time that if we suddenly discover new evidence to suggest that apples are carcinogenic, we are likely to affect not just the demand for the health attributes of apples but of many other goods as well. This is a form of 'externality' the importance of which I suspect is much underestimated. Am I alone in discounting statements about what is good or bad for me in my diet because there has been so much misinformation issued in recent years by the medical profession and other 'experts' about possible harm from different foodstuffs, additives, and so on? Rightly or wrongly, I still eat butter, and if I'm told tomorrow that Guinness is not good for me, I will tend to discount the information because of all the conflicting information I have previously received on butter and margarine – and also because I like Guinness for its other characteristics as well.

But perhaps more serious is the fact that such a model tends to assume a high degree of rationality on the part of the consumer and a well-informed household. Whether such assumptions are justified must be debatable. However, these are not reasons for rejecting the notion of the household's 'health durable asset', particularly in the context of non-health-care health-producing activities, where in any case, whether we like it or not, the consumer will tend to be sovereign.

In practice many of the non-health-care health commodities around are prevention goods. Thus, while most forms of cure are vested in the formal health care system, the majority of prevention consumption is elsewhere. Some of it is organised by recognised agencies – road safety, clean air, river pollution control, and so on. Other aspects are the subject of legislation, normally, interestingly, to constrain 'bad' consumption (e.g. it is illegal to use certain drugs, to drink over a certain amount and then drive a motor vehicle; non-pasteurised milk cannot be marketed; cigarettes and alcohol are taxed to reduce the quantity demanded) rather than promote 'good' consumption (e.g. why don't we have a subsidy or negative tax on jogging shoes, wholemeal bread and polyunsaturated fats?). Again, in other instances the market and the consumer are left to get on with it.

The demand for these non-health-care health-promoting activities has been analysed by various writers (see for example Ippolito,[8] Heffley,[9] Cohen and Mooney,[10] Cohen and Henderson[11]). What is apparent is that many commodities have some either health-promoting ('preventive') attributes or health-diminishing ('hazardous') attributes. This is clear with, for example, smoke-detecting devices. But for Flora Margarine, not only does it have a nice taste on bread and toast, it also has the characteristic of being more health-promoting than its close substitute butter. Swimming is not only enjoyable as a sport, but it also promotes fitness; it also has the health-diminishing characteristic of there being some risk of drowning associated with it.

Consequently, the demand for health can be very complex. As exhibited in health care, it is subject to considerable problems of lack of knowledge and lack of rationality on the part of the consumer. Outside of health care the demand is exhibited as that for various health-promoting and health-diminishing facets of all sorts of different types of commodities. For the former we tend in society to organise the health care system in such a way as to assist and moderate consumer demand so that individuals are more likely to get it 'right' than if left to their own devices. In the equally complex world of non-health-care health-promoting/health-diminishing consumption, except where the effects are both clearly discernible and potentially disastrous (and of course that word can be subjected to all sorts of different interpretations), consumers are much more free to make their own mistakes. There would seem to be an inconsistency here.

In addition to the externality of misinformation on risk, two other forms of externality exist concerning health. There is the consideration that if you have an infectious disease, then your state of health may directly affect mine. This is an issue of much less importance today, at least in developed countries, than it has been in the past. (But it is not absent. When one of my colleagues has a cold, my suggestion that he or she take the day off and return to bed is born of concern for my being infected as well as for his/her poor health.) AIDS has clearly important externalities. Here also we have the second externality. To a greater extent than in other aspects or characteristics of our fellow beings, we do appear to be concerned for the health of others. This 'humanitarian spill-over', as Culyer has called it, [12] does seem to be an important form of externality which, while not unique to health (we can be concerned for the poor, for example), is more pervasive (we care about the rich being ill as well as the poor) and stronger (we are probably more likely to give, at the margin, to charities concerned with alleviating ill-health than those aimed at alleviating poverty). It is interesting to note that even with a national health service, as in the UK, there are still many people who donate funds and give of their time to buy dialysis machines, scanners, TV sets for hospitals, and so on. Indeed, this 'humanitarian spill-over' has been suggested as one of the fundamental reasons for the UK National Health Service being established. (More detail and discussion of this issue is in Chapter 9.)

Before leaving health I would also point to what I think is an increasingly important aspect of discussions in this area. This is the tendency to consider that health in itself is 'a good thing'. Health is clearly value-laden (something we will consider in detail in the next chapter). But what this means is that individuals may well value it differently and make different 'trade-offs' between different aspects of health. Some people, for example, may prefer a short and handicap-free life while others would opt for longer life even if this was with some handicap or other.

These considerations are very much concerned with values. And this needs to be recognised. At the same time there is a need to accept that in 'advocating' health or healthy life-styles there may be some disadvantages to this in terms of increasing individuals' anxiety levels. For example, cholesterol lowering policies may result in reduced heart disease but they may at the same time increase the level of anxiety in the population as a result of telling people what their cholesterol levels are. (For an interesting example of this, see the study by Kristiansen *et al.*[13])

3.4   Health care

The nature of the commodity health care has been examined by a number of economists in the last few years. In this section, in discussing it, I wish to acknowledge my debt to, in particular, Arrow[14] and Culyer.[15]

Economics, as discussed in the context of demand in Chapter 2, normally starts from the point of view of consumer sovereignty; that is, that the individual is the best judge of his own interest. Then there may be some relaxation of these assumptions. For example, my consumption of alcohol can have implications for others ('externalities') in that I may indulge in anti-social activities such as drunken driving. The government may then intervene and pass laws to penalise me if I drink and drive, to protect not so much myself as others. Thus, government may interfere in different ways to influence consumption decisions by individuals.

But a second problem of this type is rather important in the context of health care. There may be, as Arrow suggests,[16] and as is discussed in the context of medical ethics in Chapter 7, 'a discrepancy, real or fancied, between the decisions an individual would reach on his own and those that he should reach to increase his own welfare. In short, he may be ill informed about what is good for him.' As Arrow indicated, this is the classic paternalistic argument.

The basic point with regard to health care is that there is a major asymmetry in information between the doctor and the patient. The results of this are that first, the patient's ability to make his own decisions is impaired and second, he becomes very much dependent on the doctor to make decisions on his behalf. What is crucial is that the patient has little check on the doctor, when the doctor is determining the patient's 'need' (of which more in Chapter 6).

Part of the explanation for this, but largely a separate issue, is the fact that the demand for health care is both irregular and unpredictable. Add to this the fact that illness is not only risky (e.g. with some probability of death) but financially expensive. While some of these items of irregularity, unpredictability and high financial cost may be observed in markets for other goods, it is difficult to think of any other where they are all present.

There is also considerable uncertainty regarding the quality of the product. Not only is it difficult for the doctor to judge on many occasions the probability of a particular outcome (and obviously even more difficult for the patient) but there is the added difficulty for the patient of not being able to judge if the doctor has done a good job. This is very different from the market for avocado pears where the quality of the product is as well known to the regular consumer as it is to the producer.

The issue of the behaviour expected by the patient of the doctor is also an important consideration and arises in a sense because of all the points already made, particularly the question of differential information. However, the key factor here is not the differential information per se but rather the knowledge of both parties — doctor and patient — that the differential exists.

Arrow lists four ways in which the expected behaviour of the doctor is different from that expected of the typical businessman: [17]

1. Advertising and overt competition are virtually eliminated among physicians.
2. Advice given by the physician as to further treatment by himself or others is supposed to be completely divorced from self-interest.
3. It is claimed that treatment is dictated by the objective needs of the case and not limited by financial considerations.
4. The physician is relied on as an expert in certifying to the existence of illness and injuries for various legal and other purposes. It is socially expected that his concern for the correct conveying of information will, when appropriate, outweigh his decision to please his customers.

It is interesting to note that while the nature, organisation and financing of health care systems differ in many respects between countries, as far as I can judge, while Arrow was writing specifically about the US health care system, all of his points appear valid to other health care systems as well. Further, we may note that given these circumstances, it is hardly surprising that even in the USA the profit motive in health care is comparatively weak (with many more not-for-profit than for-profit hospitals).

Turning more directly to the supply side, there are a number of features of interest in health care markets in comparison to normal competitive markets. Clearly, entry to the medical profession (as is true of many others) is restricted. This results in raising both the quality and the cost of medical care.

A related phenomenon on the supply side is that restriction of entry results in a restriction in the *range* of quality. In many markets it is possible to find varying quality (and normally, therefore, price) for particular types of commodities. But this is much less marked in medicine. Clearly, however, there have been some attempts to substitute less highly trained (and hence less costly) personnel for some tasks previously undertaken by medical staff.

In normal markets, prices play an important role. In health care their influence is usually muted, although in some instances it can be enhanced. For example, the greengrocer cannot discriminate in prices between rich and poor, but under at least some health care systems such price discrimination by income is both possible and practised. Pricing policy also comes into play in terms of doctor remuneration where in different countries, and sometimes even in the same country, doctors can be paid salaries on a per capita basis or on a fee-for-service basis.

But perhaps the most significant aspect of all on pricing policies in health care in all countries is that price competition, which is normally seen as a virtue in other markets, is considered a vice. It is deemed 'unethical' for the medical profession to indulge in price competition.

The existence in many countries of some form of health insurance also affects the 'market' for health care. Once the premium is paid, then prices at the point of consumption are either zero or heavily subsidised, with the inevitable consequences of higher quantities of health care demanded than would otherwise be the case.

Given these problems on both the demand and the supply side for the commodity of health care, it is not surprising that markets for health care tend to be rather different from markets for other commodities. Indeed, the way that health care is supplied varies markedly from country to country, even within the industrialised West, stretching on the one hand from the UK *National* Health Service to the more market-orientated system of the USA, from salaried systems for the medical profession to fee-per-item of service, from zero money prices at the point of consumption (indeed, even 'negative' prices as incentives for taking up services, e.g. for ante-natal care in France) to substantial co-payment by consumers, and so on.

There is no general agreement on how best to deliver health care. Indeed, it is striking that while medical technology knows no boundaries in the sense that it is genuinely international in its availability and consumption, that is not true of the technology of health care delivery. We are much more ignorant about other countries' systems of health care than we are about their medical technology. Even where we have some knowledge, we struggle to form judgments about the relative value of different systems.

But this is changing. More countries are reforming or considering reforming their health care systems. As a result there is a growing recognition that we can learn from how other countries organise their health care. These issues are ones we will return to in Chapter 9.

3.5 Conclusion

A number of points emerges from this chapter; for example, that the nature of health care will vary depending on the way in which health care is organised and financed. This may in turn be a function of ideological and cultural variations between countries. The method of remuneration of the medical profession will also have major implications for the demand and supply of health care.

It is clear, however, that while no single feature or characteristic of health care is unique to health care, there are few if any goods which have *all* the characteristics of uncertainty, irrationality, unpredictability, large monopoly elements, paternalism and important externalities. To those who doubt that health care is different the question must be posed of why it is that it gets *treated* differently from lawnmowers, transport, education, books, and so on.

Indeed, it is the combination of all these factors which makes health care unique as a commodity. Within these factors, perhaps the most important is the knowledge gap between patient and doctor and, perhaps even more significantly, what might be termed the 'knowledge squared gap' – the knowledge by both parties that the knowledge gap exists. As is discussed in Chapter 7, it is this which largely explains the existence of medical ethics, and it is this which almost wholly explains the importance of medical ethics.

Another important issue which emerges from this chapter is the question of how we are to grapple with the problems of measuring and valuing health. This we discuss in the next three chapters.

Notes

1. I am grateful to Croom Helm Ltd for permission to reproduce a few passages from my chapter on 'Values in Health Care', in *Economics and Health Planning*, ed. K. Lee (Croom Helm: London, 1979).
2. World Health Organisation, *Official Records No. 2* (1948).
3. J. Kosa and L. Robertson, 'The social aspects of health and illness' in *Poverty and Health*, eds J. Kosa *et al.* (Harvard University Press: Cambridge, Mass., 1969), p 35.
4. A.C. Twaddle, 'The concept of health status', *Social Science and Medicine*, 8 (1974), p 31.
5. *Ibid.*, p 30.
6. M. Grossman, 'On the concept of health capital and the demand for health', *Journal of Political Economy*, 80 (1972).
7. *Report of the Royal Commission on the NHS* (HMSO: London, 1979).
8. P.M. Ippolito, 'Information and the life cycle consumption of hazard goods', *Economic Inquiry*, 19 (1981).
9. D.R. Heffley, 'Allocating health expenditures to treatment and prevention', *Journal of Health Economics*, 1 (1982).
10. D.R. Cohen and G.H. Mooney, 'Prevention goods and hazard goods: a taxonomy', *Scottish Journal of Political Economy*, 31 (1984).
11. D.R. Cohen and J.B. Henderson, *Health, Prevention and Economics* (Oxford University Press: Oxford, 1988).
12. A.J. Culyer, *Need and the National Health Service* (Martin Robertson: London, 1976).
13. I.S. Kristiansen, A.E. Eggen and D.S. Thelle, 'Cost effectiveness of incremental programmes for lowering serum cholesterol concentration: is individual intervention worth while?', *British Medical Journal*, 302 (1991).

14. K.J. Arrow, 'Uncertainty and the welfare economics of medical care', *American Economic Review*, 53 (1963).
15. A.J. Culyer: 'The nature of the commodity health care and its efficient allocation', *Oxford Economic Papers*, 23 (1971); 'The normative economics of health care finance and provision' in *Providing Health Care: The Economics of Alternative Systems of Finance and Delivery*, eds A. McGuire, P. Fenn and K. Mayhew (Oxford University Press: Oxford, 1991).
16. K.J. Arrow, 'Government decision making and the preciousness of life', in *Ethics of Health Care*, ed. L.R. Tancredi (National Academy of Sciences: Washington, DC, 1974), p 35.
17. *Ibid.*, p 949.

4

Health status measurement

> A nail factory met its target of 100 tons of nails by
> fabricating nails of 1 kilo each. The planners saw their
> error and instructed the factory to maximize the number of
> nails. The nails were too small to be of use.
>
> H. Oxley, 'Rainbows and pots of gold: the search for
> public sector efficiency', Public Sector Workshop:
> Helsinki (1991)

4.1   Introduction

Health status measurement and valuation are two of the most
important and most difficult aspects of health care evaluation
generally and of health economics in particular. Essentially, measurement is difficult for three reasons: (1) health is a value-laden
concept, (2) health is multi-dimensional, and (3) it is normally not
enough to be able to measure health ordinally, we need cardinal
measurement.

Ordinality and cardinality (on both an interval and a ratio scale)
are discussed in this chapter before considering two approaches to
the measurement of health status. The first example emphasises the
need for different judgments − both technical and value judgments
− by different 'actors' in the health care system.[1] The link (and
sometimes confusion) between ordinality and cardinality is highlighted and the way that an index can be used is exemplified.

Second, the questions of 'QALYs' and their measurement are set out at some length. These represent a particular form of health status measurement that have gained some popularity (and notoriety!) in recent years. This is an area of research which is both vast and multidisciplinary. In one short section it is not possible to do justice to all that has been done, even by restricting attention to the efforts of economists. However, and fortunately, there are various review articles of health status measurement and of QALYs; these are recommended for the reader whose appetite is whetted by this issue (see Drummond,[2] Mooney and Olsen,[3] McDowell and Newell[4] and Torrance[5]).

4.2 Some issues in measuring health

One of the main problems in any health care evaluation is that of measuring health or health status and changes therein. The problem is not peculiar to economic evaluation, and many people from different disciplines have turned their minds to the issue. Different types of approach have been adopted and different types of health indicator devised. Before considering an example, some general comments are worth making about health status measurement.

There are potentially many uses to which health indicators can be put. For example:

1. To compare the health status of the populations in different countries and relative changes through time.
2. To compare the relative health status of the population in different regions of a country; for example, in order to form judgments about the allocation of health service expenditure to different regions.
3. To measure the effects of different forms of clinical practice.

Different types of indicator will be relevant depending on the use envisaged. This in turn raises two important aspects of health status measurement: first, the fact that it is value-laden and, second, the related issue of the dimensions to be adopted in measuring health in specific contexts. On the former, Pole has remarked:[6]

> A health status index is, on the face of it, a means towards
> transferring the emphasis in decision-making on health care policy
> from the plane of political judgment to the plane of scientific
> evaluation, but this presupposes that the arguments underlying the
> construction of such indices are substantially technical rather than
> moral. This is far from being the case.

This issue of being value-laden is of importance regarding the
choice of dimensions since that choice should be made on the basis
of ensuring that what is measured allows one to see the extent to
which the objective of the policy is being pursued. For example, if
in care of the elderly, health status is measured in terms of life
expectancy alone, this implies that health policy in care of the
elderly is concerned solely with keeping the elderly alive. (Clinicians
are perhaps the biggest sinners in this respect. In cancer-control
programmes, for example, despite various recent efforts to improve
the position, it remains too often the case that the measures of
health status they use are restricted to mortality.) If, however, a
prior statement is made that health policy in care of the elderly has
the objective of assisting the elderly to function as well as possible
in terms of social intercourse, looking after their own personal
care, and so on, then measurements of health status might then be
couched in terms of ability to go out of doors (alone, with aid, not
at all), ability with personal care (able to wash alone, able to wash
with aid, unable to wash), and so on. There are also different
methods of indicating states of health. These broadly fall into two
categories: ordinal and cardinal. An ordinal ranking system means
simply that certain states of health are deemed to be better than
others and, consequently, some are deemed to be worse than
others. Thus, a health status index for the elderly would rank 'able
to get out and about without an aid' as a higher (better, less severe)
status than 'able to get out and about, but only with an aid', and
'able to get out and about, but only with an aid' as a higher (better,
less severe) status than 'not able to get out and about at all'. If we
ascribe numbers to these health statuses, with a high number denoting a good health status and a low number denoting a poor health
status (it could be the other way about if we wanted), then we might
have the following ordinal ranking:

1 = not able to get out and about

2 = able to get out and about, but only with an aid
3 = able to get out and about without an aid

Then 1 is worse than 2, 2 is worse than 3 and, of course, 1 is worse than 3. Notice that such an ordinal ranking says nothing about how much worse 1 is than 2 or how much better 3 is than 2. While such an ordinal scale can be a useful starting point, ideally in most instances we would want to operate with 'cardinal' scales so that we have some measure of the *difference* between points on the scale.

Essentially, there are two types of cardinal scales: interval scales and ratio scales.

On an interval scale, the numbers ascribed to health statuses not only indicate ordinal ranking but also that the interval between the numbers is the same. Thus, if the example of the scale for the elderly above were an interval scale, then we could say that to improve someone's health status from 1 to 2 would be as good as improving someone's health status from 2 to 3. We could not, however, say on an interval scale that it was three times better to have health status 3 than to have health status 1. To help grasp this, note that temperature is measured on an interval scale: thus, a change in temperature from 50°C to 60°C is equal to a change from 70°C to 80°C, i.e. both involve an increase of 10°C. However, it is not legitimate to argue than 80°C is 'twice as hot' as 40°C or that 100°C is 'hundred times as hot' as 1°C. This is clear if we switch to Fahrenheit: the former is a change from 176°F to 104°F; the latter from 212°F to 33.8°F. The reason why interval scales do not permit this 'X times' comparison is simply because the zero is fixed arbitrarily and has no meaning in itself. On a ratio scale, not only are the intervals between the numbers the same but also we can say that a health status of 10 is twice as good as a health status of 5 and five times as good as a health status of 2. (Distance is measured on a ratio scale: thus, ten metres is twice as long as five metres and five times as long as two metres.)

Different methods can be devised for arriving at different scales of health status. Essentially, however, in deciding whether a particular health status is better or worse than another (i.e. ordinal ranking), this involves a value judgment (which might, given the practical problems involved, have to be determined by a doctor, whether or not in principle this was thought to be the best source of values.) Deciding how much better or worse (i.e. introducing cardinality) clearly involves another value judgment, and one which is much less likely to be the prerogative of the medical profession and which is more of a social judgment.

Let us consider an example. Someone with a cold, *ceteris paribus*, has a lower/poorer health status than someone without a cold. Someone with pneumonia, *ceteris paribus*, has lower health status than *either* someone without either pneumonia or a cold or someone with a cold. These statements involve both value and technical judgments.

Now, let us say that it is possible to cure a cold at a cost of £50 and to cure pneumonia at a cost of £1,000 (the cost difference being twenty times). If only £1,000 is available, should we treat 20 colds or one case of pneumonia? If we value the change in health status from 'pneumonia' to 'no pneumonia' more than twenty times as highly as the change in health status from 'cold' to 'no cold', then we would treat the pneumonia case; if not, we would treat the colds. But deciding whether or not it is twenty times as bad to have pneumonia as having a cold is a value judgment.

Culyer spells out the following technical characteristics of a good health status index:[7]

1. It should be reliable and *reproducible* by different persons.
2. It should be valid in the sense that it should measure what it purports to measure.
3. It should be capable of being related to some of the variables over which the researcher, practitioner, administrator, etc. has some control.

4.3   An example

In this section I want to set out how one study proposed to construct a health status measure. In many respects it is an 'ideal' index of health and as such it may be that it is not possible to conduct this measuring process as fully or as well as that ideal would require. We are dealing with something here that really is very difficult. However I think it useful to see how these researchers (Culyer, Lavers and Williams[8]) set out to tackle health status measurement. (While the article is now old, I have retained it in this revised edition because nowhere have I been able to find a more modern article which covers the relevant issues as well as this.)

When considering the summary of the work by Culyer and his colleagues as set out here, I would ask those readers who may be somewhat sceptical of the processes suggested to bear in mind four things. First, resources for health care are scarce. Second, this means that choices have to be made. Third, if rational choices are to be made then it is necessary to be able to compare the outputs of different ways of using scarce resources if we are to maximise the benefit to society with the health care resources available. Fourth, choices are currently made and even if we cannot get to the sort of perfection that this section (and perhaps also the next) points to, surely we can do better than what is currently done in measuring outputs from health care.

Culyer and his colleagues state that they are interested in measurement of health primarily from a health care policy point of view.[9] At the same time, they emphasise that the appropriate nature of a health index is very much a function of its purpose. They thus claim that 'indicators which are to be of use in the formulation of policy must take account of the preferences of society and the costs involved in accommodating these preferences'. By this stage of this book these types of comment will be becoming familiar. They are none the less worth emphasising.

Culyer and his colleagues suggest that decision-makers require three types of indicator: (1) an indicator which is really about how much of what is being produced, (2) one covering the value to be attached to this production, and (3) one about how the production is to be arranged. Notice that all three are required. The impression gained very often in health services is that it is really only (1) and (3) which are necessary, but this would require the assumption that all needs can be met. (We'll come back to this in Chapter 6.)

In developing the first of these, their 'State-of-Health' index, the authors emphasise the need to combine medical and social judgments; that is, to use medical judgments to assess or describe various health states together with social judgments about the weights to be attached to these different health states.

The issue of 'multi-dimensionality' is crucial in health status measurement. If there were no such thing as morbidity and we were all either simply dead or perfectly alive, then health status could be measured purely in relation to mortality. However, morbidity does

exist and in a vast number of different forms and dimensions. The
ideal in health status measurement is to convert all these dimensions on to a uni-dimensional scale. It is hardly surprising that this
is proving difficult to achieve!

Figure 4.1 (reproduced from Culyer *et al.*[10]) is a reflection of the
medical judgments about what it is like (in terms of pain on the
vertical axis and restriction of activity on the horizontal axis) to
suffer from certain medical conditions, the examples in the diagram
being conditions o, Δ and ×. Notice that both the scale of degree
of restriction of activity and the scale of painfulness are ordinal
scales (e.g. 'confined to house and immediate vicinity' is better than
'confined to house' but no indication is given of how much better;
similarly for 'mildly uncomfortable' compared to 'very uncomfortable'). Thus condition o is judged to be less painful and less
restrictive of activity than condition Δ or condition ×.

Regarding Figure 4.2, also reproduced from Culyer *et al.*,[11]
Culyer and his colleagues state that this 'pairwise comparison is
essentially a social judgment and should be recognised as such, but

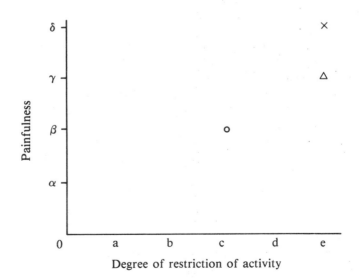

Figure 4.1 Medical conditions classified by painfulness and
degree of restriction (Source: A.J. Culyer, R.J. Lavers and A.
Williams, 'Social indicators: health', *Social Trends: No. 2*
(HMSO: London, 1971))

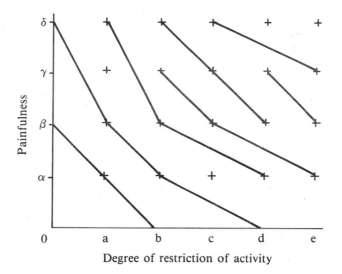

Figure 4.2 Contour lines of combinations of pain and restriction (Source: Culyer, Lavers and Williams, *op. cit.*)

may have to be made in practice by medical people'. The point here is that while it can be argued that it is rightly a medical judgment regarding what it is like to be in a particular state, once two states are being compared, relative weights are then being attached to the two states. In other words, judgments are being made about whether more importance (and hence by implication more of society's resources) is to be attached to avoiding one state as compared to the other. This is clearly a value judgment which strictly speaking goes beyond the technical competence of doctors. Nonetheless, it may be that for practical purposes no one but doctors is in a position to form these value judgments.

What is afoot in Figure 4.2 is worth emphasising. Each combination of pain and degree of activity is a description of a state of *ill*-health. In making the 'pairwise comparison' three possible judgments are:

1. Combination (A) is worse than combination (B).
2. Combination (A) is the same as/equivalent to combination (B).
3. Combination (A) is better than combination (B).

Where a line is drawn joining two combinations, this means that they are judged to be equivalent (e.g. δb and βd). Painfulness increases the higher up the vertical axis we move, and there is increased restriction of activity the further to the right we are on the horizontal axis; thus, the further to the 'north-east' we are from the origin, the worse is the combination indicated by any line.

One way of considering these lines is to say that there is a disutility associated with being in a state of ill-health; or conversely, there is some utility associated with moving from these states of ill health to the origin (i.e. no pain, no restriction). For those combinations of pain and restriction of activity for which the gain in utility is equal in moving from them to 'no pain, no restriction', then they can be assumed to be equivalent and are joined up by an equivalence line.

Perhaps this is an appropriate point for a reminder that we are not in a fantasy world with all this and that, despite the difficulties involved in assessing such matters as the intensity of pain and how it compares from one person to another, none the less doctors can and do already make such assessments and comparisons.

Culyer and his colleagues then introduce a cardinal scale of the ratio type (e.g. state 9 is three times as bad as state 3). It is therefore not simply about the rank order of the conditions but also about the weights attached to them. This means that because weights are used, value judgments are involved in deciding the relative importance of avoiding one state as compared with others.

Now, if we add duration into this process, we can begin to use the procedure to look at the impact, in terms of effectiveness, of health care treatments. Thus, we can examine examples of a particular type of case and ask the following questions:

1. What is the time profile of the health status for a case of this type if it is not treated? (Figure 4.3.)
2. What is the time profile of the health status for a case of this type if it is treated? (Figure 4.4.)

Now, since the scale of health status being used is such that one week at health status 4 is equivalent to two weeks at health status 2 or half a week at health status 8, it is legitimate to calculate the areas under the lines in Figures 4.3 and 4.4 in terms of what might be termed 'health status week' points. The objective is to try to minimise the number of health-status-week points (given the

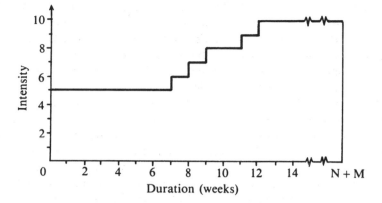

Figure 4.3 Time profile of health status − no treatment

constraint on resources available, of course). We clearly want to minimise these points because the scale is couched in terms of high numbers being bad (e.g. 10 = death) and we want any pain/discomfort/disability, and so on, to be for a shorter rather than a longer time.

A glance shows that the area under the line in Figure 4.4 is very much smaller than that under the line in Figure 4.3; that is, the treatment is effective. To quantify this effectiveness (i.e. the 'output' of the treatment) and the third index proposed by

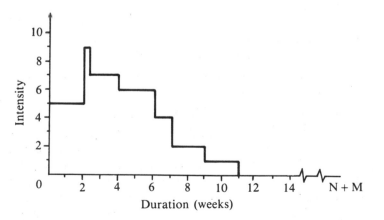

Figure 4.4 Time profile of health status − with treatment

Culyer and his colleagues and discussed above (see page 39), we have to subtract the area under the line in Figure 4.4 from that in Figure 4.3. Over time, in the first two weeks, the patient is in the same health state whether or not he is treated (or, more accurately, to be treated); in the third to sixth he is worse off being treated than he would have been had he not been treated; only in the seventh week and after is he better off under treatment.

4.4 Quality Adjusted Life Years ('QALYs')

One way of trying to grapple in practice with health status measurement as discussed in the context of the approach by Culyer *et al.*[12] in the previous section is through the use of QALYs. Seen from a health economics standpoint, QALYs represent one of the most controversial developments in health care evaluation in recent years. They have provoked much debate. Here I do not want to further the debate but rather to try to set out clearly what QALYs are about. However, at the end of this chapter I will try to give an overall appraisal of QALYs and their potential for helping in the development of efficient health care and perhaps also (but much less so in my view) equity in health care.

First, what are QALYs? They are a form of health status measurement which attempts to place mortality and morbidity on the same measuring rod. What is their function? In essence QALYs have two main functions (although it is possible to extend this to many others which have in my view lesser importance). First, they can allow more informed and rational judgments to be made about the effectiveness of one form of treatment for a particular problem as compared with another treatment for that same problem. Clearly, in economic terms, to be able to do so allows judgments to be made about X-efficiency (as spelled out in Chapter 2). Is conventional surgery more efficient than laparoscopic cholecystectomy? Further, there are clear advantages in using this form of economic appraisal, 'cost-utility analysis' (CUA), as compared with cost-effectiveness analysis (CEA), because CUA allows more than one type of outcome to be included, whereas CEA is restricted to a uni-dimensional measure of outcome.

But more controversially QALYs can be used in helping to judge relative priorities across different programmes in health care.

Different types of treatment for different problems can be compared on the basis of 'marginal costs per QALY gained' and the programmes with the 'cheapest' QALYs given highest priority. (This is on the basis that with a fixed budget for health care, the goal is to maximise the number of QALYs within that budget which in turn means buying the cheapest ones first.)

It is for this purpose that the 'QALY league tables' have been devised. (See for example Table 4.1.) A few words of caution with regard to these tables are appropriate. First, their full title ought to be 'Marginal cost per QALY gained league tables' – which is clearly a bit of a mouthful but has the advantage of being somewhat more accurate as a description of what these tables contain – or at least ought to contain. Second, one of the key implications of the tables and indeed of QALYs generally is that the only output of health services is health. That seems a rather narrow view and there is a danger that in adopting it, health economists are allowing the medicalisation (or more accurately the 'doctorisation') of health economics. In other words, medical doctors seem all too ready to believe that the only output of health services is health; there is no reason for economists to accept this without more evidence from the consumers that that is what they want – or, more accurately, that health is all that they want. Third, another implication of QALY league tables is that the resource use that these tables examine only have opportunity costs in terms of QALYs. In other words, the only outcomes possible and the only foregone outcomes

Table 4.1 A QALY league table

Intervention	Present value of extra cost per QALY gained (£)
GP advice to stop smoking	170
Pacemaker implantation for heart block	700
Hip replacement	750
GP control of total serum cholesterol	1,700
Kidney transplantation (cadaver)	3,000
Breast cancer screening	3,500
Heart transplantation	5,000
Hospital haemodialysis	14,000

Source: Adapted from M. F. Drummond, 'Output measurement for resource allocation decisions in health care' in *Providing Health Care: The Economics of Alternative Systems of Finance and Delivery*, eds A. McGuire, P. Fenn and K. Mayhew (Oxford University Press: Oxford, 1991).

from the resources that are considered in these tables are health outcomes. If the resources involved are not used to purchase QALYs in one way, their only alternative uses are with respect to purchasing QALYs in some other way or ways. That is clearly a bit of a problem if we look at resources − as we should − which are involved in health care production but which fall outside the health service budget. In particular it means that other social services' resource use in support of health service programmes is difficult to incorporate in QALY league tables. Further, the resource input − very often largely time − of the patients is not, and indeed cannot legitimately be, included in such league tables. Finally, if equity is to be measured in terms other than health − and we will discuss some other possibilities in Chapter 8, such as access or utilisation − then it is clear that QALY leagues tables do not include equity. They cannot, as their only output is QALYs.

A final comment on QALYs per se is that they assume that what we want to measure is the value or utility associated with health state X, then the utility of health state Y and that the change in utility is given by the difference between these. In other words the assessment of a health state is independent of the state of health one is in when one makes the assessment. (I may feel very different about being in a wheelchair depending on whether, when I make the judgment, I am reasonably fit and well − as of now − or I am already in the wheelchair when I make the judgment.)

For a fuller discussion of some of these issues see Mooney and Olsen.[13]

Yet I begin to fall into the trap of seeming to be very critical of QALYs. However, the reader should note two things here. First, the intention in setting out these opinions is not to knock QALYs down. Rather it is to try to ensure that expectations with respect to them are realistic. Second, nearly all the reservations expressed relate primarily to the question of QALY league tables and thus the use of QALYs with respect to allocative efficiency issues. Comparing different treatments for the same health problem is where the QALY can be supported almost unreservedly. And that is no mean recommendation, given that even today so many clinical evaluations are still performed using very inadequate measures of output. It is at the 'across programme' level that more problems are created. Not that that means we should drop QALYs at this level − just be aware of their limitations in this context. (For a debate on this issue, see Donaldson *et al.*[14] Williams'[15] comment and the reply from Donaldson and Wright.[16])

Now, even if the ordering seems a little odd, I want to turn to the measurement of QALYs. I have been quite deliberate in setting the ordering thus because I have found so often that the measurement issues get in the way of the issues of principle with QALYs. If the reader becomes obsessed with the measurement issues, he or she may fail to appreciate the beauty (relatively at least!) of the principles incorporated in QALYs.

The history of QALYs is relatively long but the key names associated are first (chronologically at least!) Torrance[17] in Canada and second, Williams[18] in the UK. In attempting to measure QALYs, what is being attempted is to devise some uni-dimensional scale which will allow both mortality and various forms and severity of morbidity to be placed on this single scale and in such a way that it is possible to compare health states one with another. This is to be done in the sense of saying not just that health state X is better than health state Y (i.e. ordinally) but also how much better (i.e. cardinally). What we want to be able to do is both to add together health outputs and to compare the outputs in terms of costs per QALY from different ways of producing QALYs.

Here I want to set out, following Torrance,[19] the three main ways of attempting to devise QALYs. These are the 'visual analogue scale' or the 'rating scale'; the 'time trade-off' method; and the 'standard gamble'.

The first of these involves simply setting out a line on a page (or in some versions a thermometer) usually with one end equal to 0, equated with death, and the other end set at 1, equated with some best state of health. The idea then is to get those asked to form judgments about other intermediate states of health to say where on the line these would lie. If, for example, losing the use of both legs is seen as being at 0.75 then this means that the respondent believes that the loss of his or her legs reduces their health status *vis à vis* good health by one quarter. (An example of such an approach as used by Sintonen[20] is presented in the appendix to this chapter.)

The time trade-off method is largely self-explanatory. It involves asking respondents to establish equivalents in terms of, for example, 20 years of life with the loss of both legs followed immediately by death and X years of life with perfect health followed by immediate death. If the respondent then sets X equal to 15, then the valuation of the health state 'loss of use of both legs' where 1 is perfect health is 0.75 (as in the example above using the rating scale).

The third approach, the standard gamble, is slightly more complex and involves facing the respondent with a pair of choices. One choice is remaining in their current (less than perfect) health state; the other involves some probability (p) of being immediately restored to perfect health and some probability (1 − p) of dying immediately. The respondent is asked to vary p until he or she is indifferent between the choices. If, for a current health state of the loss of use of both legs, the individual sets p equal to 0.75, then 0.75 is the valuation of this health state (when again death is 0 and perfect health is 1).

Which of these methods is to be preferred is the subject of considerable controversy. Clearly, if they all produced the same results, then the choice wouldn't matter. Unfortunately it appears that the measurements that emerge from the methods are not independent of the measuring method.

Additionally there remains the question of who to ask. This takes us into the debate on 'whose values', which is the subject of the next chapter.

There has been a lot of debate in recent years about health status measurement, especially with respect to 'QALYs'. Much of it seems to have been about two issues. First, health status 'cannot be measured'; and second, even if it can, QALYs are rather inadequate in doing so. What may be important to bear in mind here is that clinicians and policy-makers are implicitly making judgments about health status weights and measures daily. (It is simply not possible, for example, to draw up a contract for health services in the reformed NHS without implicitly at least measuring the expected health gains from contracting for one set of services as compared with another. At least one would hope that some idea of health status gains underlies the contracting process!) Further it is unlikely that there is anyone who would consider that the science or art of health status measurement has been perfected or that QALYs are the final word. There is a long way to go before we can be really confident that we are getting acceptable measures of what we want from QALYs. What is abundantly clear, however, is that what is currently done in health services by way of output measurement is really pretty dreadful and that, for many, QALYs represent a step in the right direction.

What has to be constantly remembered in all of this is that it really is very difficult to measure health well.

Am I being too defensive about QALYs? I think not. I have been rather critical of some of the work here myself and indeed have been taken to task by some of my health economist colleagues for this. But my criticisms are not intended to be 'anti-QALYs'. They are aimed at trying to see if we can get health care outcomes measured even better than current QALYs do and at pushing away the seemingly growing view that health economics is only about QALYs. (For example, see Klein.[21]) They are also an attempt to make sure that we walk with QALYs rather than run too fast and face too much hostility, especially from the clinicians, in getting them used. There are problems and discussing them cannot do any harm − provided they are seen against the background of the need to improve on the way that health care outcomes are currently measured.

Notes

1. A.J. Culyer, R.J. Lavers and A. Williams, 'Social indicators: health', *Social Trends: No. 2* (HMSO: London, 1971).
2. M.F. Drummond, 'Output measurement for resource allocation decisions in health care' in *Providing Health Care: The Economics of Alternative Systems of Finance and Delivery*, eds A. McGuire, P. Fenn and K. Mayhew (Oxford University Press: Oxford, 1991).
3. G. Mooney and J.A. Olsen, 'QALYs: where next?' in *ibid.*
4. I. McDowell and C. Newell, *Measuring Health: A Guide to Rating Scales and Questionnaires* (Oxford University Press: Oxford, 1987).
5. G.W. Torrance, 'Measurement of health state utilities for economic appraisal', *Journal of Health Economics*, 5 (1986), p 1.
6. J.D. Pole, 'The use of outcome measures in health service planning', *International Journal of Epidemiology*, 2 (1973), p 25.
7. A.J. Culyer, *Need and the National Health Service* (Martin Robertson: London, 1976), p 33.
8. Culyer, Lavers and Williams, *op. cit.*
9. *Ibid.*
10. *Ibid.*
11. *Ibid.*
12. *Ibid.*
13. Mooney and Olsen, *op. cit.*

14. C. Donaldson, A. Atkinson, J. Bond and K. Wright, 'Should QALYs be programme-specific?', *Journal of Health Economics*, 7 (1988), p 239.
15. A. Williams, 'Comment on "Should QALYs be programme-specific?"', *Journal of Health Economics*, 8 (1989), p 485.
16. C. Donaldson and K. Wright, 'Programme-specific QALYs: a reply', *Journal of Health Economics*, 8 (1989) p 489.
17. G.W. Torrance, 'Social preferences for health states, and empirical evaluation of three measurement techniques', *Socio-Economic Planning Science*, 10 (1976), p 129.
18. A. Williams, 'Economics of coronary artery bypass grafting', *British Medical Journal*, 291 (1985), p 326.
19. Torrance, 1976, *op. cit.*
20. H. Sintonen, 'An approach to measuring and valuing health states', *Social Science and Medicine*, 15C (1981).
21. R. Klein, 'The role of health economics: Rosencrantz to medicine's Hamlet', *British Medical Journal*, 299 (1989), p 275.

Appendix to Chapter 4

This appendix was first published by H. Sintonen, 'An approach to measuring and valuing health states', *Social Science and Medicine*, 15C (1981) and is reproduced here, without adjustment, by kind permission of Harri Sintonen and Pergamon Press Ltd.

A number of characteristics have been listed below which are associated with a healthy person. Various people may have different views of what health is about and how important various characteristics are as far as health is concerned. Here we are interested in your personal view. Evaluate first which of the characteristics below is in your opinion the most important as far as health is concerned – that is, the one which you would give up last – and draw a line from the box following it ($\Box\!\!>$) to 100 on the adajcent scale. Then evaluate the importance of all the other characteristics in relation to this most important characteristic. If, for example, some characteristic is in your opinion half ($\frac{1}{2}$) as important as the most important characteristic, draw a line from the box following it to 50 on the scale. If some characteristic in your opinion is not at all important as far as health is concerned, draw a line from its box to 0. For clarity, write in each box the number at which the line drawn from the box is aimed (e.g. $\boxed{30}\!\!>$). In evaluation you may use all numbers between 0 and 100 as you see fit. The characteristics are:

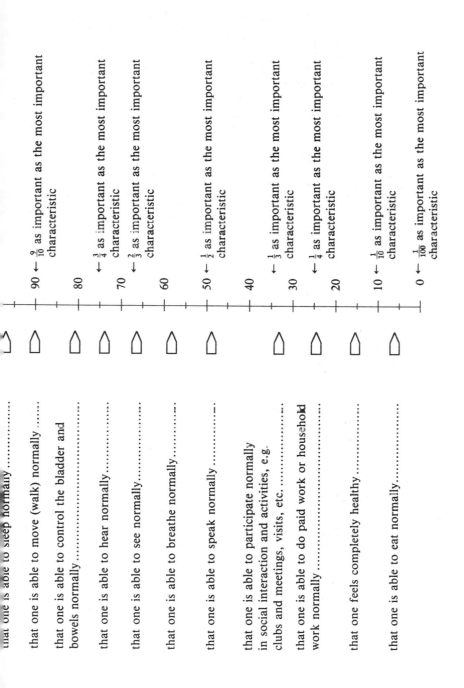

5

Values in health care

5.1 Whose values?

> In the days when investigation was non-existent and treatment as
> harmless as it was ineffective, the doctor's opinion was all that there
> was, but now opinion is not good enough ... The medical profession
> has always preferred to travel hopefully rather than to arrive,
> because arrival is often so disappointing. This habit leads to
> oscillating fashions ... Although the value of prophylactic treatment
> of infarct survivors with a beta blocker has been better investigated
> than almost any treatment for any cardiovascular problem, this
> treatment has not yet become part of routine clinical practice –
> because many doctors prefer to move on to the new and
> unproved ...

Opinion? Hope? Fashion? Exciting challenges? These notions
about how the medical profession operate are not mine, nor indeed
those of a fellow economist. They are taken from a leading article
by Professor J.R. Hampton, a cardiologist, in a paper entitled 'The
end of clinical freedom'.[1] Perhaps the comments are not surprising. Certainly I believe it is a welcome sign that some doctors
should be thinking in this way.

But how *do* doctors decide? Indeed, what should doctors
decide? Jennett, the former Dean of the Medical Faculty in
Glasgow has written:[2]

> the lack of generally available predictive criteria about many of the
> conditions requiring rescue leaves many clinicians feeling that they

have to treat all patients as though they had potential for recovery ... A consensus on the principles which should apply to rescue triage should be reached not only amongst doctors in one clinical team or discipline, but should also involve other doctors, as well as health administrators and others whose task is to monitor hospital activities. Unless there is agreement about such principles, individual doctors may not have the courage to take the rational rather than the traditional decision when faced with a rescue situation.

There has to be room for improvement – and understanding – on how doctors make decisions. What I want to concentrate on here is one aspect of this, the issue of valuation: first, the question of whose values; second, the question of how we elicit values from the relevant valuers; and lastly, the question of how we might use one particular approach, that of 'implied values', in practice.

This is the area of health economics which is most disturbing for most health care professionals. To be trained in medicine, nursing or one of the other 'sharp end' disciplines and then be faced with some hard-nosed, cold-blooded economist placing money values on human life and suffering is anathema to many. Maybe it is no help to know that we have no choice as to whether we do this valuing or not; our only choice is whether to do it explicitly and thereby better or implicitly and almost certainly badly.

Let's get the issue of the inevitability of the process sorted out first. Returning to some of the basic principles of economics discussed in Chapter 2, if I decide to buy an avocado pear priced at £1, from this behaviour you can immediately tell that I value an avocado pear at at least £1, otherwise I wouldn't buy it. If, additionally, I refuse to buy an avocado pear when it is priced at £1.10, then you can judge that I value an avocado pear at between £1 and £1.10. Thus, faced with costs of consumption, our behaviour can tell observers quite a lot about the value we place on the benefits we get from our consumption. In other words, through these 'implied values' we reveal our preferences by our behaviour.

The same is true in principle in health care, even if it is not always the consumer who is doing the valuing. Thus, as indicated by Gould,[3] the fact that the British government in 1971 apparently refused to spend £1,000 per life saved on the child proofing of drug containers suggests that they were valuing a child's life at less than £1,000. Moving outside health care but still in life-saving, the decision of the US Environmental Protection Agency to implement particularly stringent environmental standards for control of smoke into the atmosphere suggested, according to Pearce and his colleagues,[4] a cost per life saved at the margin of at least $110,000.

Such decisions cannot be avoided; consequently, such valuing is inevitable. But even if it is inevitable, does that necessarily make it desirable that we attempt to make those values explicit? Death itself is inevitable – but, given the taboos that surround it, that does not mean that it is necessarily good for us to think about it explicitly, or at least not too often.

The example of air pollution quoted above points to why it may be desirable on grounds of economic efficiency and hence of health promotion to make these values explicit. In the study by Pearce and his colleagues no attempt was made to argue in 'absolute' terms that a certain level of air cleanliness was 'needed' or was 'a good thing'. The issue as they perceived it was quite simple: given certain assumptions, spelled out as best one can, how does spending on life-saving in this area of environmental protection compare with the return on similar spending elsewhere? In other words, do we save more lives if we spend on environmental protection of the atmosphere or on road safety or health care? They produced a table of comparative implied values of life in different life-saving programmes (see Table 5.1).

It should be emphasised that it does *not* automatically follow, taking the data in Table 5.1 together with the $110,000 implied value of life in the smoke reduction standards, that spending on reducing air pollution is a bad thing. *If* the effects of all the programmes listed were wholly comparable – that is, the lives saved

Table 5.1 Implied values of life in various health care policy areas

Policy area	Implied value of life ($)
Pulmonary embolism	19,000
Renovascular disease	25,000
Heart attacks:	
Ambulance	6,000
Mobile coronary unit	8,300
Triage plus ambulance	27,000
Screening	46,000
Critically ill patients	24,000 (per year of life)
End-stage renal disease	24,000 (per year of life)

Source: D. Pearce *et al.*, 'Rational establishment of air quality standards', *Environmental Research Perspectives*, 52 (1983).

were similar, the morbidity effects the same, other effects (e.g. damage to crops) the same – then we could say categorically that on the criterion of economic efficiency air pollution reduction is not the best buy. It would be better to invest in the other activities first. Alternatively, it would be possible to argue that reducing air pollution to the extent that current US standards do is excessive, but less stringent standards might compare well with the other programmes listed.

Thus, presenting such cost data and thereby implied values explicitly helps the decision-making process. It certainly does not make the decision. To do that requires consideration of the weight to be attached to economic efficiency (*vis-à-vis*, for example, equity), of the assumptions used and of whose values are to be deemed relevant in making the decisions.

The answer to the question of whose values in health care, will depend on many factors. Prime among these are what type of health care system we are considering, what types of health care we are examining and why we are asking the question.

In 'normal' market economics, economists usually assume that the knowledgeable consumer is the one whose preferences are to count; that is, the concept of consumer sovereignty, as discussed in Chapter 2, applies. When we examine the markets for health care, as we discovered in Chapter 3, the situation in all countries, whatever the organising and financing of health care, looks rather different.

How relevant is consumer sovereignty in health care? Is conventional economic demand theory (as spelled out in Chapter 2) appropriate?

If consumer sovereignty is to apply, then, as I have discussed elsewhere,[5] three questions have to be answered in the affirmative:

1. Does the individual accept that he is the best person to judge his own welfare?
2. Is the individual able to judge his own welfare?
3. Does the individual want to make the appropriate judgment?

Let us look at these three questions in some detail. Question 1 essentially concerns whether the consumer believes in consumer sovereignty in principle in health care. This relates to the underlying ethics as seen by the consumer, an issue to be debated in Chapter 7. Or is he more inclined to the view that his own preferences are so likely to be wrong that the principle of consumer sovereignty in the context of health care should be broken — indeed, that that is the very reason why we train a medical elite?

Going back to the discussion in Chapter 3 of the nature of health and health care and to our three questions on consumer sovereignty, it seems very likely that in health care the individual's manifest preferences and his true preferences will not be the same. It is thus the case that the separation by Harsanyi of these two types of preference is very relevant in health care.[6] Whether his conclusion holds, that social utility should be based on manifest preferences, I will discuss under the question of whether the individual wants to make the appropriate judgments. Consequently, in answer to our first question I think we can safely say that the principle of autonomy should apply to the issue of whether the individual accepts consumer sovereignty for himself or not. The answer to that question will very likely depend on the cultural and health care system setting in which it is posed, of which more in Chapter 9.

Adopting this stance allows us to retain the economist's God of rationality. As Harsanyi has described, 'This concept of rational behaviour arises from the empirical fact that human behaviour is to a large extent goal-directed behaviour. Rational behaviour is simply behaviour consistently pursuing some well-defined goals, and pursuing them according to some well-defined set of preferences or priorities.'[7] Within this it is quite rational to argue as individuals that in principle the most rational stance for us to adopt on values is to accept that we are not well placed by ourselves to get our manifest preferences to coincide with our true preferences. We need help; we need an agent acting on our behalf (an issue discussed more fully in Chapter 6).

But then, turning to our second question, is the individual able to judge his own welfare? Against the background of the discussion in Chapter 3, the answer here must surely be 'in many situations, no'.

As I have suggested elsewhere:[8]

> Attitudes to health care and to health ... are such that the individual
> may have great difficulties in understanding the likely effects of
> different forms of treatment and even if he does may still be unable
> to evaluate the disutility and/or utility associated with different
> health states ... There may be some sort of continuum which
> stretches from conditions about which the relevant utility and

disutility parameters are very well known to the patient, to others about which he knows little or nothing. This continuum may well be matched by one which reflects a complete ability to form the necessary judgments about the value of health care to complete lack of ability ... This in turn will be reflected in a valuation system which stretches from the one pole of consumer sovereignty to the other of imposed 'merit goods'.

(A 'merit good' embodies the notion that some elite is better placed than individuals to form judgments about what individuals' preferences ought to be.) I think the above quotation gives an accurate description. But it carries with it a problem in that it requires not only an ability to measure values under these very different bases but also an awareness of which applies to what policy questions and what level of mix is appropriate in differing circumstances.

What about our third question, which we have already touched on in Chapter 3? It might seem that by answering the first we would have the answer to the third, but that does not necessarily follow. The process of choice may have a value in itself; the utility here can be a function of, for example, our belief in individual autonomy, our concern about getting decisions right (or failing to get them wrong) *additional* to the outcome of getting it right and our desire to blame others if the decision is wrong.

Freedom to choose does not necessarily have a positive utility attached to it. It may be negative. If I want *not* to make the decision ('Doctor, I can't decide. What do you think?') to be forced to do so diminishes my utility, even if the outcome in terms of the impact on my health status remains the same. There is an important ethical issue here which I will discuss in Chapter 7.

A related and potentially important issue is the question of what might be described as autonomous externalities. If I believe in freedom of choice for myself, this may influence my neighbour to believe similarly. Clearly, with many issues my beliefs may influence my neighbour's and vice versa. But I would argue that, in the context of a principle such as this, it is often the case that as individuals we positively seek support for our principles in our neighbours, friends, colleagues, and so on.

But these autonomous externalities may take a less passive form. Crudely, this has been expressed in the political slogan 'people should stand on their own two feet'. The relevance to our discussion here is that this view is expressed about not just the speaker but about others and indeed it is often directed specifically and explicitly at those who appear unwilling to accept this dictum. In other words, freedom of choice is deemed to be 'a good thing' whether individuals want to choose to have freedom of choice or not. (There are also equity considerations here since one individual's ability to choose may well be different from another's – but that is another issue.)

Clearly, the value system on which any health care service is based is exceedingly complex and indeed constitutes potentially a series of systems which may vary across different commodities within health care and across different cultures and time periods. Thus, the basis of how we value health and health care is a cultural and changing phenomenon which cannot be, or at least ought not to be, seen in a vacuum, as it were, and separate from other concerns of governments and nations. For example, Rothschild writing about welfare activities generally suggests that the issue of freedom of choice/individual autonomy may be a more important driving force in influencing the health care value system than the level of spending: [9]

> There is ... no alarming evidence that welfare activities have reached a stage where the 'too much' problem is evident. The present backlash against 'welfarism' cannot be supported by clear-cut evidence of harmful economic effects. It is partly the result of a wave of conservative and middle-class sentiments which highlight the importance of 'personal success' and take elitist and restrictive views on social policy, and partly a consequence of widespread economic, inflation and budget problems which have fostered a demand for retrenchment policies.

At the present time the move seems to be to more and more consumer sovereignty in health care mixed with concern about promoting more and more efficiency. Unfortunately, these two are becoming confused and, indeed in some people's minds, synonymous. This is unhelpful, particularly when the medical profession appear by and large to be part of the trend towards greater individual autonomy in health care. In fact, they may be leading it. Given that they are not neutral about the outcome of the current great debate about health care and that they are a potent force within all health care systems, their behaviour may be of paramount importance in determining the outcome. As three leading

Canadian economists have written: 'Providers hold the key to the dynamics of the health care market.'[10] It is at our peril – whether we are considering the supply side of the market or the demand side – that we ignore this fact.

5.2 Valuing outputs

To value outputs in health care is technically difficult; to defend doing so is morally easy. Most readers, insofar as they have thought about this issue at all, have perhaps had difficulty with the morality and glossed over the technical problems. As indicated (see page 55), the explicit valuing of health outputs promotes economic efficiency, and economic efficiency promotes health. Morally, then, that position is defensible. (This should not be confused with the moral dilemma that it throws up; essentially, whether it is morally right that somebody, somewhere should *explicitly* decide who shall live and (the opportunity cost) who shall die. I am sympathetic to those health service decision-makers who worry about this issue. But the costs of avoiding it are too high. For those who do not like it, it may be that they need to be replaced by those more prepared to play the grizzly algebraic game of *y* chronic renal failure patients given *x* years' more life versus *z* cases of psoriasis treated successfully.)

It is not, however, central to this book that the reader has a detailed knowledge of how health outputs are valued. (For more information on this see Linnerooth,[11] Mooney[12] and Jones-Lee.[13]) Briefly, there are three methods commonly encountered. First, there is the implied-values approach already discussed (see pages 53–5). This has the merit of being based on the existing decision-making procedures and value structure of health care. Essentially, it 'teases out' the values implied by past decisions. Insofar as these emerge as being very different from one another, then for similar outputs at the margin of different programmes they can be used to examine whether some X-inefficiencies are present; that is, if the implied value of life in one programme is £1 million and, for similar lives, in another it is £10,000, there is inefficiency present in that a shift of funds from the first programme to the second would result in an overall gain in lives saved. (Ideally, we want to move to the position where the marginal implied values of similar outputs are the same in all programmes.)

If the values that emerge for the same marginal output in different programmes are similar, then these may be used in evaluating new programmes which come up for examination. Unfortunately, little work has been done on this approach to date. What has been done suggests that the implied values emerging, for values of life at least, vary markedly.

A second approach, and indeed the most commonly encountered, equates the value of life with the value of livelihood. This human capital approach suggests that man may be valued in terms of his productive output, the valuation of which is equated with his earnings (or more accurately the labour costs of employing him which will usually be greater than his earnings), discounted through time and adjusted to allow for expected participation in the labour force. In the context of health care it may be argued that this at least provides 'floor' values since *one* objective of health care is to get people back to productive employment. Insofar as there are other objectives, the value emerging has to be a minimum. Clearly, there are major problems with this omission of non-work values, particularly as it leaves the valuation of pensioners and many women at worst at zero and at best problematical. Perhaps its main virtues are its ease of applicability and the fact that it does allow relevant market outputs to be valued.

A third approach is that of consumer demand: essentially, attempting to determine how much individuals are prepared to pay to reduce their risk of death or morbidity from some existing low level to some still lower level. Thus individuals faced with a risk of death of, say 3 in 1,000 might be asked how much they would be prepared to pay to reduce this to 2 in 1,000. If on average 1,000 individuals said £200, then the 'value of life' would be £200,000 (i.e. £200 × 1,000). This 'willingness to pay' or 'WTP' approach is currently the one most fashionable among economists primarily because it satisfies their concern with consumer sovereignty. But then, given the discussion in Chapter 3 and earlier in this chapter, it is far from clear that consumer sovereignty based values – at least unadulterated ones – are appropriate in health care valuation. (For an interesting example of the use of WTP see Donaldson.[14])

What should we do in practice? Beyond attempting to improve the methodology of valuation, perhaps the most sensible approach at the present time is to adopt the implied-values method. It requires the least stretching of the health care decision-makers' imagination and credence, which, in the short run at least, is perhaps the best criterion to adopt. If economists wish to appear credible as analysts generally in health care, then in this particular arena a little cautious tip-toeing is justified.

What must be emphasised is that the issue *cannot* be avoided. That is the crucial message. It is a message which is explicitly spelled out in the implied-values approach. So in the short run at least, perhaps we should leave it there, except to add that the emphasis placed on different value systems ought not to be treated as exogenous. *What* is to be valued − that is, what the objectives and outputs are − and *how* values are derived may be influenced by agents within health care. For example, in another context, but he might have been writing about doctors in health care, Majone suggests that 'rational policy actors do not take the institutional framework as given, but pursue their self-interest also by devoting resources toward obtaining favourable institutional changes'.[15] He further underlines this by stating that 'Since very concrete regulatory decisions may depend on basic philosophical attitudes, it is not surprising that policy actors allocate resources toward altering societal values and beliefs.' This broad issue is one we will return to in the last chapter of this book.

5.3   Measurement by implied values

Given the emphasis in this chapter on implied values, this section presents a method of weighting health status which is based on this approach. (The idea is spelt out in more detail in Hurst and Mooney.[16]) The implied-values approach is essentially what is more often referred to in economics as revealed preference, the idea that as individuals our behaviour reveals our wants, desires and the relative weights we attach to them. (If you observe my difficulty in deciding whether to spend £1 on either two avocado pears or four oranges, then this behaviour reveals that I give twice as much weight to an avocado pear as to an orange in my preference function. In other words, the utility I derive from an avocado pear is twice as great.)

This approach has been extended from the individual to organisations (see McFadden[17]). Indeed, it has been suggested as a means for weighting health statuses.[18] As indicated previously (see page 53), every time an individual or an organisation chooses to devote resources to a particular end, that reveals something about his or its preferences. When an organisation has multiple outputs then by studying the way that it allocates resources to produce the different outputs this can help to indicate the relative weights it attaches to the different outputs – assuming that it is 'in equilibrium'. (In this context this simply means that the decision-makers are broadly happy with the mix of outputs they are achieving, given the resource constraints that they face.)

This whole approach is based on cost-benefit analysis (discussed in detail in Chapter 2) and can be exemplified as follows. In circumstances where there is no budget constraint and a single output from a particular programme then the decision on how far to allocate resources to that programme should be based on equating marginal cost and marginal benefit. So, for example, assuming we can measure and value all relevant costs and benefits in money terms, then in programme A in Table 5.2 the optimal output, if there is no budget constraint operating specifically on programme A, is 6 units of outputs. At this point marginal cost and marginal benefit are equal (at £10). If a seventh unit is produced, the benefit of that unit (£5) is less than its cost (£10). Consequently, given the cost-benefit approach, applied here at the margin, the optimal output is 6 units. What happens if we have two programmes and not enough money available to reach this point of marginal benefit equal to marginal cost in both? How do we decide how much to spend on each programme? On efficiency grounds the answer is clearly to maximise the benefit of both programmes combined. Let us look at an example of this, again assuming that both costs and benefits are capable of being valued in money terms. Programme B in Table 5.2 is concerned with a different policy area to that of Programme A (e.g. a different group of patients). Now, if there were no budget constraint specifically on programme B, then it should be producing 5 units of output since at that level both marginal cost and marginal benefit equal £20.

If the total expenditure available for programmes A and B together is £100, how can we allocate it out? Table 5.3 gives some possible combinations. Of these the best buy is 4 units of A and

Table 5.2 Marginal costs and marginal benefits in two programmes

Unit of output	Programme A				Programme B			
	Marginal costs (£s)	Total costs (£s)	Marginal benefits (£s)	Total benefits (£s)	Marginal costs (£s)	Total costs (£s)	Marginal benefits (£s)	Total benefits (£s)
1st	10	10	35	35	20	20	60	60
2nd	10	20	30	65	20	40	50	110
3rd	10	30	25	90	20	60	40	150
4th	10	40	20	110	20	80	30	180
5th	10	50	15	125	20	100	20	200
6th	10	60	10	135	20	120	10	210
7th	10	70	5	140	20	140	0	210
8th	10	80	0	140	20	160	0	210

Table 5.3 Possible allocations of a total expenditure of £100

Programme A		Programme B		Total (A + B)	
Units of output	Benefit (£s)	Units of output	Benefit (£s)	Total benefit (£s)	Total cost (£s)
8	140	1	60	200	100
6	135	2	110	245	100
4	110	3	150	260	100
2	65	4	180	245	100
0	0	5	200	200	100

3 units of B since this combination gives the greatest total benefit for £100. Looking back now at Table 5.2, at these levels of output what we find is that the ratios of marginal benefit to marginal cost in each of the programmes are the same; that is, £20/£10 in A and £40/£20 in B. This gives us the decision rule that benefits are maximised when the ratio of marginal benefit to marginal cost is the same in all programmes.

Now, that is the theory. In practice it is very difficult, indeed perhaps impossible, to measure all the benefits and costs in money terms. Does this then mean that the approach breaks down? No, we simply start at the other end. If costs can be measured and decisions *are* taken, then implicitly at least the benefits are being valued or weighted.

Thus, in the example above, if benefits were not capable of being valued but costs were, then we could observe that marginal costs were in the ratio of 2:1 and therefore if the decision-makers were getting it right, that marginal benefits must be in the ratio of 2:1 at the margin. In other words, in practice we have the decision determining the level and we have (normally) a fairly accurate assessment of costs. The benefit weights then 'drop out' of the analysis.

Little effort appears to have gone into using this approach to elicit weights attached to different health outputs at different levels of decision-making. Perhaps the most obvious place to start is at the clinical level where clinicians do have to decide how best to allocate their time and resources across the needs and demands of their various patients. Given the difficulties in deriving health status indices and valuing outputs, this approach has the merit of having a very pragmatic ring to it. That may be no small blessing in an area of research where good empirical work is like an oasis in a vast conceptual desert.

5.4 Que faire?

So what do we do about values, valuers and valuation in health care? The messages emerging from this chapter are simple. First, it is not for economists to determine what the bases of the value systems in health care should be nor who the valuers should be, although we can point to the implications of different choices. Second, attempting to determine what these bases are is important and economics can help with that. Third, whatever the bases, making the values in decision-making explicit can only be good for any health service, good in the sense of leading to increased efficiency. Again, economics can clearly assist with this.

Too often it seems health service decision-makers are not aware of the extent to which value judgments enter into their decision-making. Additionally it would seem important to provoke a debate about the appropriateness of different actors' value judgments at different levels of decision-making matter. Perhaps this chapter has helped to highlight some of the issues here. The next takes the process further and suggests how some of the different values can be partially reconciled.

Notes

1. J.R. Hampton, 'The end of clinical freedom', *British Medical Journal*, 287 (1983) p 1237.
2. B. Jennett, 'The cost of rescue and the price of survival' in *Clinical Practice and Economics*, eds. C.I. Phillips and J.N. Wolfe (Pitman Medical: Tunbridge Wells, 1977), p 54.
3. D. Gould, 'A groundling's notebook', *New Scientist*, 51 (1971).
4. D. Pearce, G. Mooney, R. Akehurst and P. West, 'Rational establishment of air quality standards', *Environmental Health Perspectives*, 52 (1983).
5. G.H. Mooney, 'Values in health care', in *Economics and Health Planning*, ed. K. Lee (Croom Helm: London, 1979).
6. J.C. Harsanyi, 'Morality and the theory of rational behaviour' in *Utilitarianism and Beyond*, eds A. Sen and B. Williams (Cambridge. University Press: Cambridge, 1982).
7. *Ibid.*, p 42.
8. Mooney, *op. cit.*, p 29.
9. K.W. Rothschild, 'Observations on the economics, politics and ethics of the Welfare State', *Zeitschrift für die gesamte staatswissenschaft*, 138 (1982), p 575.

10. M.L. Barer, R.G. Evans and G.L. Stoddart, *Controlling Health Care Costs by Direct Charges to Patients: Snare or Delusion?* (Ontario Economic Council: Toronto, 1979), p iv.

11. J. Linnerooth, 'The value of human life: a review of the models', *Economic Inquiry*, 17 (1979).

12. G. H. Mooney, *The Valuation of Human Life* (Macmillan: London, 1977).

13. M.W. Jones-Lee, ed., *The Value of Life and Safety* (North Holland: Amsterdam, 1982).

14. C. Donaldson, 'Willingness to pay for publicly-provided goods: a possible measure of benefit?', *Journal of Health Economics*, 9 (1990), p 103.

15. G. Majone, 'Institutional choice and social regulation: the case of environmental and occupational health standards' (International Institute of Applied Systems Analysis: Laxenburg, 1981).

16. J.W. Hurst and G.H. Mooney, 'Implicit values in administrative decisions' in *Health Indicators*, ed. A.J. Culyer (Martin Robertson: Oxford, 1983).

17. D. McFadden. 'The revealed preference of a government bureaucracy: theory', *Bell Journal of Economics*, 6 (1975).

18. Hurst and Mooney, *op. cit.*

6

Need, demand and the agency relationship

6.1 Introduction

The concept of 'demand' was discussed in Chapter 2 and that of 'need' mentioned in Chapter 3. In this chapter some of the key elements of demand, need and the relationship (where it exists) between them are highlighted. There is a now vast and still expanding literature on this broad area, and it is not intended that any sort of comprehensive survey of existing research be presented. Rather some aspects which were raised earlier are now brought together.

Economists, as the reader will now be aware, are wont to argue that the issue of values in health care is of major importance. Further, they suggest that the criteria for choosing which 'actors' perform which 'roles' in the valuation process ought to be made much more explicit than is often the case in current health service decision-making.[1] Indeed, it is possible in this book to introduce the reader to only a little of the material written about the nature of the commodities health and health care, about the problems of market failure, about the extent to which any conventional economic theory of demand is relevant to health care, about the nature and relevance of the concept of need and the role, in theory at least, of the agency relationship in health care supply and demand. For those who wish to pursue this particular topic in more detail, Arrow,[2] Culyer,[3] McGuire *et al.*[4] and Williams[5] are especially recommended.

Culyer draws attention to two non-economic approaches to the supply of health care, as outlined by Fuchs. First there is the *'romantic'* who is an individual who 'fails to recognise the scarcity of resources relative to wants'.[6] The romantic approach leads to virtually no analysis taking place because if one fails to recognise or appreciate that resources are scarce and that choice is necessary in deciding what wants/needs are to be met and which left unmet, then there is little need for analysis or evaluation. Second, there is the *'monotechnic'* who fails to recognise 'the multiplicity of human wants and the diversity of individual preferences'.[7] This approach again does not encourage analysis. Many doctors appear to be either romantics or monotechnics.

The economic approach embraces both the notion of scarcity (and is therefore unromantic) and the fact that the wants of society are many and varied (and is therefore polytechnic). Culyer points up one of the central problems of health care when he states, in the specific context of the UK National Health Service, although the point is more generally true, 'Pervading the whole system, there has been the pretence that many problems are financial, management or technical problems, whereas they are often, if only in part, value problems; and the consequence has been that big questions concerning whose are the values that should count have been left unposed and ... unanswered.'[8] Having gone over the issue of 'whose values?' in Chapter 5, there is no need to repeat the debate here.

6.2   Demand and the need for health care

As was discussed in Chapter 2, economists tend to assume in the context of conventional demand theory that consumers are well informed, and able and willing to make their own decisions regarding their consumption behaviour. In other words, the sovereign consumer chooses to exercise his sovereignty by making explicit, rational choices between different goods and services in order to maximise his utility. Given the nature of health care (as outlined in Chapter 3) and the question mark raised about the role of consumers' preferences in Chapter 5, there have to be some doubts about the relevance of conventional demand theory in health care. In particular, uncertainty and lack of information are likely to create difficulties in applying demand theory in an unadulterated form to the commodity of health care. But this does not mean that demand is of no assistance in analysing health care. What needs to be resolved is the debate in Chapter 5. In other words, what is the extent and nature of the departure needed from conventional demand theory in the health care sector?

Grossman, whose ideas were aired earlier in Chapter 3, argues that the consumer does have enough information to be able to make rational choices about his health both currently and in the future.[9] He suggests that the individual's demand for health care is derived from his perception of his optimal level of health. The demand for health care consequently arises because the individual wants to bridge the gap between his perceived current health state and some higher health state that he desires. As a result of this desire, one course of action – others are clearly possible – is for the individual to decide to seek health care.

At the other end of the spectrum it is possible to view the consumer as being much less knowledgeable than Grossman assumes. He may be ignorant about both current and future health states, the range and effectiveness of treatments available, and so on. In such a view of the patient's position it is the doctor who both supplies the necessary information to make rational choices and makes the decision about which treatment and to what extent is required for the particular health state of the patient, as diagnosed by the doctor.

This 'needs' approach is based on the notion of 'merit goods', introduced in Chapter 5, and reflects the judgments of some elite – in this case, medical doctors who either impose their judgments on the patients or have their decisions accepted by the patients. (The jargon of 'merit goods' has come in for some justified cynicism from one economist, Margolis, who suggests that a merit good is 'any item of public expenditure that seems socially reasonable but cannot be accounted for within the ordinary economic theory of demand. It is a kind of formalised escape clause'.[10])

Clearly, the concept of need conflicts with that of consumer sovereignty. Yet it would be wrong to place consumer sovereignty on a pedestal. There will be occasions when some correction or even replacement of ignorant consumers' preferences will be justified. Certainly, as Chapter 5 indicated, there has to be some debate about who should formulate the relevant valuations. In practice in health care, need does creep in but seldom to the complete exclusion of demand.

It can also be argued that the *need* for health services is a function of the need for health per se. In a sense this is self-evident. Yet in much of the debate about 'need', this simple notion of the need for health care being a 'derived' need — that is, derived from the need for health — tends to be lost sight of.

One thing that clearly emerges from the different views of 'need' is that in using the word we must be very careful to convey precisely what it is that we mean. Indeed, in some debates about health care policy one is occasionally left with the feeling that use of the word 'need' is designed deliberately to confuse the listener and to stifle rational thought and debate. ('We *need* a new hospital': end of story.) For economists, 'need' is an evaluative, normative notion which has some kind of objective lying behind it.

It is all too easy in considering 'need' to assume that if a treatable condition exists, therefore (1) it should be treated and (2) it should be treated in the 'best' way possible, 'best' here being defined as 'medically most effective'. If this were accepted, this would mean that all need should be treated and only the most effective treatments should be used. Both of these ignore the facts that resources are scarce and an overall better use of resources may be obtained from employing less effective but cheaper policies.

Doubts about the relevance of demand lead to the view that ideas of value (and hence of need) may be more suitably elicited from people other than the consumers themselves. This is part of the reason why some economists, like Williams and Anderson,[11] prefer to talk about a 'marginal value curve' rather than a demand curve. With a demand curve it is assumed that the consumers are doing the valuation (i.e. that consumer sovereignty is operating). In the case of a marginal value curve the question of who is doing the valuing is left open. If it is the consumers, then the demand curve and the marginal value curve are synonymous. In practice, since the commodity of health care is not homogeneous — a general-practitioner consultation is very different from treatment in intensive care — the degree to which need or demand is appropriate will tend to vary with the service being discussed.

In any debate about total need, what has to be emphasised is that not all need can be met and that there will be a 'ranking' of needs in the sense that, *ceteris paribus*, we would prefer one need to be met rather than another (e.g. if the former yielded a higher benefit than the latter). But the *ceteris paribus* assumption may not hold. In particular, it may not hold with regard to cost. Given the concept of opportunity cost, clearly it is the case that the choice of what needs to meet should be in part a function of the costs involved – and that, in meeting need, not necessarily the most effective mechanism should be adopted. Further, the extent to which particular needs are to be met will again be a function of both benefits and costs of doing so, strictly marginal costs and marginal benefits. Need is not absolute and finite. It is dynamic and tends to grow through time – and of particular interest, its growth is at least in part a function of the growth in supply of health care facilities.

Indeed, it is important that the morality of recognising that need is not absolute and cannot be met in full is accepted. As Culyer states, 'we must of necessity choose from among those moral things we think we ought to do in order to devise the best "package" in light of what is possible. Of necessity, this requires us to trade-off one need against the other. Not only, therefore, *do* we do this trading off, but it is logically inescapable and, ethically, completely legitimate'. [12]

At this point let us pick up again on the study by Culyer and his colleagues (introduced in Chapter 4) since it deals with the issue of need, linked to the question of health status measurement. [13] In introducing their discussion of need they state:

the agent responsible for the [policy] decisions (the 'Minister') should attach explicit *valuations* to a variety of levels of the state indicator [i.e. the index worked out in Ch. 4]: increments in these could then be compared with the incremental social cost of attaining any given level. Essentially, this procedure amounts to the calculation of an *intensity of need* measure which states the intensity with which 'Society' needs each of a variety of states of health.

Their approach is built round a few diagrams and it is on these that I want to concentrate here. (Some readers may find this a little daunting, but the arguments should be clear.) First of all, let us consider the notion of a 'production possibilities curve' (see Figure 6.1, set out here in the context of health and education.)

The 'production possibilities curve' shows what different combinations of education and health are possible with a given fixed

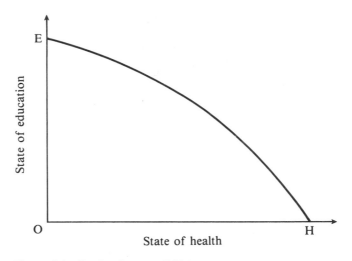

Figure 6.1   Production possibilities curve

budget. (This is shown as the curve from E to H in Figure 6.1.) Thus, if the whole budget is spent on education, there will be OE education produced and no health output; if it is all spent on health, there will be OH health produced and no education output. The points along the curve between E and H show the various combinations of health and education outputs that are possible from the fixed budget available. The curve thus indicates the trade-offs between education and health; that is, the opportunity costs of increased health are put in terms of 'education output forgone'.

In Figure 6.2 the idea of the convex 'isowelfare' curves W_0, W_1, W_2 and W_3 may again be a little off-putting to some readers. Let us take W_0 first. Notice that W_0 passes through the point H. This means that, if it is 'the Minister' who is making the judgments, he judges that all the various combinations of health and education outputs along the curve W_0 are equally as satisfactory as OH health and no education. Thus, moving upwards from H along W_0, initially he will be prepared to give up quite a lot of health to get some education. (I think we could all agree with this; if the current education budget had all been transferred to health, we would then be prepared to give up quite a lot of health output to get *some*, even small, education output.) However, as we move up the curve, giving up more and more health, we will be less and less ready to

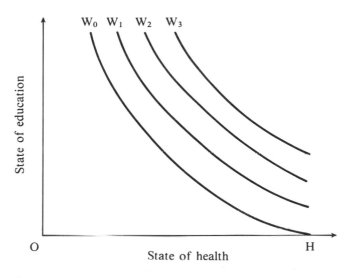

Figure 6.2 Isowelfare curves

forgo health outputs for education outputs. Indeed, by the time we get to the top of the curve, we would want a relatively large increase in education output to forgo even a little health output. This explains why these 'isowelfare' curves are convex.

Thus, each combination of output of education and health on W_0 is equally preferred by the 'Minister'; that is, he is 'indifferent' between the different combinations on W_0 (hence the economists' expression 'indifference curves'). All the combinations represented on W_1 are combinations about which he is again indifferent; this is similarly true for W_2 and W_3. The reasons are quite simple. Any point on W_1 involves more health output *or* more educational output *or* some combination of more health output and more education output than any point on W_0. *All* points on W_0 are equally desirable, and *all* points on W_1 are equally desirable. *Ceteris paribus*, more health is desirable *and* more education is desirable. But *some* points on W_1 involve both more health and more education than some points on W_0 and no points involve less of both. Consequently, W_1 is preferred to W_0, and so on for the other W curves.

Now, given the production possibility curve for a given fixed budget and the set of welfare curves W_0, W_1, W_2 and W_3, the place

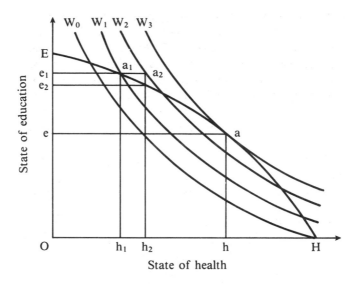

Figure 6.3 Maximising welfare subject to a budget constraint

to be is on the highest welfare curve possible for the budget available. This is point *a* (Figure 6.3), where the production possibility curve just touches a welfare curve. (Note here that a_1 is on the production possibility curve and in that sense is possible. However, it is 'inferior' because it lies on W_1 as compared to *a*, which lies

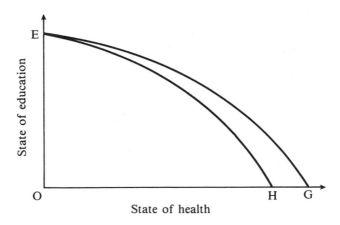

Figure 6.4 Production possibilities under changing technology

on the higher welfare curve W_3. Point a_2 is not possible since it lies outside the production possibility curve – and as it happens is on a lower welfare curve than a.) In Figure 6.4 what is happening is that because of some advance in medicine (say new technology) it is now possible to obtain more health than previously without necessarily sacrificing education. This means that the production possibility curve is pushed outwards on the health axis to the new curve EG. This is then brought together with the isowelfare curves in Figure 6.5.

Notice in particular, from Figure 6.6, that increased productivity in the health care sector will not necessarily mean that the resources freed will all be spent on more health, but some at least may go to other sectors.

Thus in Figure 6.6, it might be assumed that the changing technology in the health care sector would lead to a move from a to b_1 but in fact higher welfare can be achieved by a move to b involving some extra addition to both health and education.

The central implication of all this is that the cost-benefit approach, essentially the weighing up of costs – opportunity costs – and benefits, offers the most comprehensive method of coping with the problems raised in devising and using social indicators and measuring and using the concept of 'need'. The figures here may look rather daunting. If they prove difficult to follow, it is none the

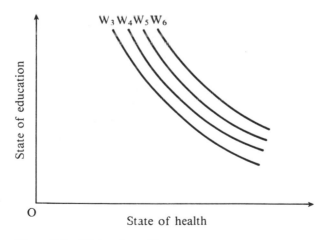

Figure 6.5 Higher isowelfare curves

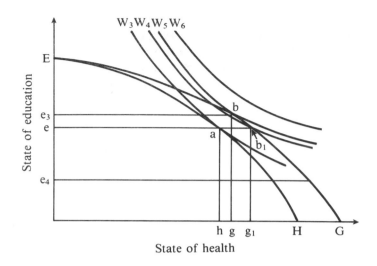

Figure 6.6 New higher welfare with budget constraint

less important to try to pick up the general principles involved, which are:

1. There is an opportunity cost of producing more health (which is shown here in terms of educational benefits forgone).
2. Some possible combinations of health and education will be preferred to others.
3. What is sought is to obtain the most preferred combination from the resources available.
4. Improved technology/increased productivity in the health care sector will not necessarily lead to any resources freed all being spent on health.
5. Generally, the concept of 'need' is useful if it is couched in cost-benefit terms where trade-offs are made explicit.

If the reader can see his way to grasping these points, then that is sufficient for the purposes of this book. Certainly, the concept of 'need' is difficult to grasp. Consequently, it may be helpful to list some key ideas about it:

1. There is a lot of confusion and illogical thinking about and surrounding the concept of 'need', sometimes perhaps deliberate in an attempt to stifle debate.

2. 'Need' ought not to be determined without considering what the end is that is being sought and to which the services in question are instrumental means.
3. Ignoring the possibilities for substitutability in meeting needs is likely to lead to problems in breeding inefficiency.
4. Almost always, no matter how need is defined, it embraces the idea of some third party being involved in the valuing process – unlike 'demand', where it is the consumer who is sovereign.
5. Which third party is relevant and which decisions are the key issues in the need/demand debate.
6. Need is not absolute.
7. Needs have to be ranked and should be costed.
8. The particular contribution of economics to 'needology' derives from the proposition that the degree to which any given need will be met will depend upon the costs and benefits of meeting it.

Both the concepts of 'demand' and 'need' are potentially of assistance in analysing and evaluating health care policy and, more importantly, the implications of different patterns of health care. The concept of 'demand' retains the basic feature of the individual's own assessment of benefits. On the other hand, the concept of 'need', provided it encompasses some assessment of effectiveness, the potential for considering alternative ways of meeting need and to differing extents, and acceptance of resource constraints, can also form the basis for resource allocation. It will normally be best for both need and demand to be taken into account when a particular operation of a health service is being examined; neither demand nor need by itself is likely to provide a sufficient basis for decision-making. Unless an effort is made, first to resolve the issue of the sometimes conflicting values on the benefit side and, second, to incorporate relevant information on costs, resource allocation in health care is likely to remain less efficient than it otherwise might be.

6.3   The agency relationship

The relationship between demand and need is clearly a complicated one. It can be argued that:

1. As individuals, we all frequently have 'wants' for better health.
2. Some of these wants we do nothing about; for others we actively seek medical care (e.g. we attend the GP's surgery).
3. The medical practitioner may not agree with us in our assessment of either wants or demands; some of our wants or demands he may argue do not need treatment or there may be certain aspects of better health which we have not included in our wants or demands which the medical practitioner believes should be treated.

These factors have been presented diagrammatically by Cooper as in Figure 6.7.[14]

I would want to quibble slightly with Cooper's layout. Certainly, the source of all demand is want, although not all wants become expressed as demand. Certainly, some wants and demands end up being judged to be needs, but not all needs are contained in demands or wants. There is thus a source of need which is independent of either want or demand; that is, members of the medical profession may define a particular need which is included in neither want nor demand.

Better, I think, to view want, demand and need as in Figure 6.8. Thus, need may be:

1. Demanded and wanted.
2. Undemanded and wanted.
3. Undemanded and unwanted.

WANT	DEMAND	NEED
An individual's own assessment of his health state. His 'want' for better health.	Those of his wants that the individual converts into demand by seeking the assistance of a medical practitioner.	A state of health assessed as in need of treatment by a medical practitioner. Not all demands will become needs and not all needs will find expression as demands.

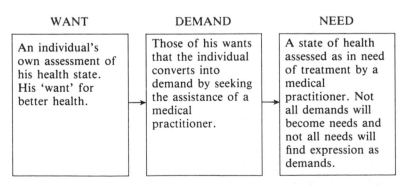

Figure 6.7 Cooper's wants, demands and needs

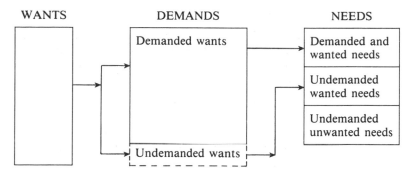

Figure 6.8 Wants, demands and needs revised

Demanded and wanted needs are likely to have a higher value than undemanded and wanted needs in the minds of the patients (presuming that it is the higher priority wants which are more likely to be expressed as demand) but not necessarily in those of the medical practitioner. Undemanded and unwanted needs are likely to have a lower value (indeed, are of zero value in their current state of knowledge) in the minds of consumers than either demanded, wanted needs or undemanded, wanted needs, but again this will not necessarily be the case for the medical practitioner. Indeed, without empirical data we have no way of ranking the priority that the medical practitioner will attach to the three types of need. The same case from a medical viewpoint could fall into each of the three types. For example, a woman with a malignant neoplasm of the breast might be any of the following:

1. She may want treatment but, not realising how important it was to be treated, not bother to go to her GP (wanted, undemanded need).
2. She may want treatment, demand it, and get it because the GP agrees that treatment is needed (wanted, demanded need).
3. She may not want or demand treatment because she does not realise anything is wrong (unwanted, undemanded need).

Can need and demand be reconciled? One way of doing so is through the 'agency relationship' in which the doctor acts as the agent of the ill-informed patient. Such a relationship exists largely because of the information problems identified in Chapter 3, leading to the view that it is the doctor rather than the patient who frequently does the demanding.

For the relationship to operate efficiently, as Artells-Herrero indicates, three sets of information are required:[15]

1. Basic medical knowledge; that is, the type of information patients characteristically are not expected to have, consisting of specialised knowledge for assessment of health status and identification of feasible treatments.
2. Descriptive information about patients' circumstances, which may involve knowledge of patients' symptoms, their medical history and environmental circumstances, and which allows the doctor to apply his more general knowledge to the patient's particular case. In addition, the descriptive information also refers to the financial position of the patient and the resources at his command.
3. Information about the patient's own valuations that include individual preferences with regard to alternative treatments, his attitude to risk-bearing and his valuation of likely trade-offs between different dimensions of well-being, such as relief from pain at the expense of a reduction in certain attributes affecting life-style, or accepting additional, present discomfort for the sake of the increased probability of avoiding future illness.

In essence, what we have here is an attempt through the agency relationship to improve on the cost-benefit calculus that the patient would otherwise have to make. Consumption choices normally involve the consumer in weighing up the costs and benefits involved and then making a decision. Problems arise in health care because the consumer will normally not bear all the costs (because of third-party financing) and may have poor perception of those he will have to bear; he will have little information about the benefits he is likely to receive from different courses of action; and in such circumstances he may be loath to take on the responsibility of decision-making. The agency relationship then acts as a process to bring together the cost-bearing, benefit-receiving and decision-making aspects of the cost-benefit calculus.

It is easy to recognise that to have a perfect agency relationship is far from straightforward. The doctor will be well placed to judge the effectiveness of different forms of care. He may find it more difficult to judge the relative benefit to the patient of such effectiveness. More problematic still will be the estimation of costs by the doctor, not only those falling on the patient but more generally. Add in a fee-per-item of service system of remuneration for doctors and the difficulties are compounded since the doctor's financial interests are then directly embodied in the decision-making process.

Beyond this individual patient–doctor agency relationship, there is the wider (and not wholly separate) agency relationship which the doctor (or perhaps clinical team) operates on behalf of the group of patients for which he or they are responsible. Here, as Artells-Herrero indicates, 'the decision-makers have to take into consideration the relative efficiency ... of devoting more or less resources to one patient *vis-à-vis* another. Implicitly they are faced with ... the comparison of the benefits arising from different patterns of resource deployment'. [16] Here the agency relationship has become concerned with priorities within the group and, indeed, social priorities. In turn that raises the question yet again of whose values are relevant to which situations (about which, more in Chapters 7 and 10).

Finally, in attempting to sum up the need/demand issue, I can do no better than quote from a paper by Williams which for me puts the issues involved in a very succinct way: [17]

> if economists insist on textbook notions of demand as the only
> proper way to go about assessing priorities in determining the
> amount and distribution of goods and services such as medical care,
> then they will miss important elements in the situation and (rightly)
> be discredited and disregarded by policy-makers. If through appeal
> to complex notions of externalities and merit goods they attempt to
> go beyond this simplistic interpretation of demand, they will be
> forced to unravel the same tangled skein of conflicting roles and
> judgments that the 'needologists' have been grappling with, and on
> which we economists have tended to pour scorn.
>
> The heart of the matter is a societal judgement as to who shall
> play what role according to which rules. The parties in the 'who' bit
> are (i) patients and other potential beneficiaries, (ii) 'experts', (iii)
> politicians and (iv) the electorate at large. The roles to be played are
> 'advertisers', 'applicants', diagnosers', 'priority-setters',
> 'treatment-assigners' and 'researchers'. The rules consist of terms of
> reference and behavioural norms to guide choice within whatever
> area of discretion is so assigned.

Notes

1. A. Williams, 'Need – an economic exegesis' in *Economic Aspects of Health Services*, eds A.J. Culyer and K.G. Wright (Martin Robertson: London 1978).
2. K.J. Arrow, 'Uncertainty and the welfare economies of medical care', *American Economic Review*, 53 (1963).
3. A.J. Culyer, *Need and the National Health Service* (Martin Robertson: London 1976); 'The normative economics of health care finance and provision' in *Providing Health Care: The Economics of Alternative Systems of Finance and Delivery*, eds A. McGuire, P. Fenn and K. Mayhew (Oxford University Press: Oxford, 1991)
4. A. McGuire, J. Henderson and G. Mooney, *The Economics of Health Care* (Routledge and Kegan Paul: London, 1988).
5. Williams, *op. cit.*
6. Culyer, 1991, *op. cit.* p 1.
7. *Ibid.*, p 2.
8. *Ibid.*, p 3.
9. M. Grossman 'On the concept of health capital and the demand for health', *Journal of Political Economy*, 80 (1972).
10. H. Margolis, *Selfishness, Altruism and Rationality: A Theory of Social Choice* (Cambridge University Press: Cambridge 1982).
11. A. Williams and R. Anderson, *Efficiency in the Social Services* (Basil Blackwell and Martin Robertson: Oxford and London, 1975), p 39.
12. Culyer, 1991, *op. cit.*, pp 16, 17.
13. A.J. Culyer, R.J. Lavers and A. Williams, 'Social indicators: health', *Social Trends: No. 2* (HMSO: London, 1971).
14. M.H. Cooper, *Rationing Health Care* (Croom Helm: London, 1975).
15. J.J. Artells-Herrero, 'Effectiveness and decision-making in a health planning context: the ease of outpatient ante-natal care', unpublished M. Litt thesis, University of Oxford, 1981.
16. *Ibid.*, p 61.
17. Williams, *op. cit.*, p 41

7

The inefficiency of medical ethics

A doctor's got to do, what a doctor's got to do.
(with apologies to the late – and great – John Wayne)

7.1   Introduction

I have been intrigued for some years by the apparent concern about economics exhibited by many members of the medical profession. There is something about the two disciplines that makes economics and medicine difficult bedfellows. It cannot be that they share a lot of common ground, which is perhaps the rather crude explanation as to why there tend to be tensions between economists and accountants. Nor is it that economists and medical doctors are in some kind of power struggle, as seems so often the case with doctors and nurses. So why?

I think the answer may lie in the different ethical bases on which the two disciplines are founded. Certainly, medical ethics is important to the medical profession and to health care. Any threat to medical ethics seems capable of being interpreted as a threat to the professional status of doctors and perhaps even to their professional integrity. It is these and related issues I want to discuss in this chapter.

A disclaimer is, however, in order. At one time I intended to write a book solely on the topic of medical ethics from an economic perspective. I quickly discovered that medical ethics was like health status measurement: a multidisciplinary industry for researchers. The literature is enormous and the disciplines involved wide and varied. Faced with spending years in learning about the area in detail, I decided to limit my concern to this one chapter (but see also Mooney and McGuire[1]) and my focus to the relationship between economics and medical ethics. Consequently, I do not intend to attempt a comprehensive description of the basis and content of medical ethics. More simply, in the wider context of the overall objectives of this book, I want to make a few observations from an economist's standpoint on the subject and practice of medical ethics. In particular, I want to highlight the uncomfortable fact that, as practised, medical ethics, particularly in the form of clinical freedom, tends to breed inefficiency. Indeed, it seems that it sometimes provides a convenient escape mechanism for the romantic member of the medical profession neither to pursue efficiency nor to attempt any rationalisation at all of the potential for pursuing efficiency in health care.

Here I want to discuss some aspects of what medical ethics is, why it exists, and some of the problems associated with it. Thereafter I will comment briefly on some of the observations by Kennedy on medical ethics[2] before discussing the appropriateness of utilitarianism as a system of values in health care.

The tensions created by medical ethics were first highlighted for me by reading an article by Muir Gray in the *Journal of Medical Ethics*[3] (to which I responded at the time[4]). Muir Gray was concerned with the problem of choosing priorities in health care. His comments, which are particularly germane, were related to the applicability and appropriateness of cost-benefit analysis and medical ethics in priority setting. There he stated that 'The strength of cost-benefit analysis, or any other concept, is a function of its weakest point, which is that it attempts to place a monetary value on human life.' This he went on to claim 'is not like the value of sheet steel, ball bearings, or any of the other commodities for which cost-benefit analysis is usually employed. It cannot be expressed in monetary terms.' He continued that the choice between treating different groups of patients 'has to be made on ethical, not on financial grounds'.

Certainly, as emerges more fully in Chapter 10, there *are* problems in applying cost-benefit analysis in health care, particularly in placing money values on the outputs (as we have already seen from Chapter 5). But in response to Muir Gray I suggested that, given scarcity, we cannot avoid valuing human life. 'The strength of cost-benefit analysis, not its weakness, lies in its ability to force consideration of the issue of placing values on health outcomes and thereby to promote the cause of efficiency in health care.'

The nub of the issue as I saw it was this. It is not a question of ethics *or* economics. Ethics is about choice; but then so is economics. Without a wider use of economics in health care inefficiencies will abound and decisions will be made less explicitly and hence less rationally than is desirable: we will go on spending large sums to save life in one way when similar lives in greater numbers could be saved in another way. The price of inefficiency, inexplicitness and irrationality in health care is paid in death and sickness.

I later discovered that Muir Gray had not intended to attack economics. Yet this exchange did seem to me to highlight the fact that among some members of the medical profession, largely through ignorance of economics, there may lurk an unhappiness and unwillingness on reputedly ethical grounds to embrace the thinking and techniques of economics. In this chapter I want to try to establish why there may be a problem.

7.2 Ethics and medical ethics

Jonsen and Hellegers define ethics as 'an academic discipline, a systematic set of prescriptions that constitute the intellectual instruments for the analysis of morality'.[5] They maintain that ethics 'provides not only a descriptive discipline of morality but a normative one as well, for its analysis purports to reveal the roots of obligation and value appreciation, thereby exposing not how men do *in fact* behave, but how *in principle* they should behave'.

Veatch suggests that 'An ethical theory is a complex, integrated approach, articulating an ethical framework coherently and systematically. The components of a complex theory of ethics will answer such questions as what moral rules apply to specific ethical cases, what ethical principles stand behind the rules, how seriously the rules should be taken, and what constitutes the fundamental meaning and justification of the ethical principles.'[6]

Beyond these broad statements it is possible to focus down on a limited number of features of ethics. There are three principal theories of ethics: the ethics of virtue, of duty and of the common good. The first two are essentially individualistic ethics and the last a social ethics.

What in turn is medical ethics? Jonsen and Hellegers suggest that 'Traditionally medical ethics has dwelt mostly within ... the theories of virtue and of duty', and they go on to state that 'the nature of contemporary medicine demands that they be complemented by the third essential theory – the common good'.[7]

In somewhat less clear tones, the British Medical Association's *Handbook of Medical Ethics* makes essentially the same point: 'As the resources available within the NHS are limited, the doctor has a general duty to advise on their equitable allocation and efficient utilisation.' It then adds: 'This duty is subordinate to his professional duty to the individual who seeks his clinical advice.'[8]

Jonsen and Hellegers claim that the lack of the ethics of the common good means that there is a lack of 'the ethical issues arising from the intersection of multiple actions in institutions and society' and that 'an adequate definition [of medical ethics] calls for an explicit reflection on the morality of institutions and the relationship, and possible clash, between social values and individual values'.[9] Perhaps the situation is changing since Veatch claims that 'Many physicians as well as lay people have opened the door to social utilitarianism in an effort to cope with the problems of traditional Hippocratic individualism.'[10] What I would want to emphasise is that I see the issue here as being one of efficiency – essentially, maximising the benefit (however defined) to society at large from the resources available (however constrained).

The purpose of the missing doctrine of the common good according to Jonsen and Hellegers is 'to consider ... how the institutional structure can be designed so as to avoid conflict, how to reconcile discord, and how to compensate unjust harm'.[11] Those are not, however, the grounds that I would stress. It is the issue of efficiency, essentially allocative efficiency, that is central to the economist's concern that the ethics of the common good should no longer be neglected and that the problem identified by these authors be overcome: 'there is little or nothing that can be identified as a doctrine of the common good in contemporary ethics of health care'.

Clearly, in medicine there are problems, first, in determining what is the common good and, second, in devising appropriate institutional arrangements to allow it to prosper alongside the individual ethics of virtue and duty. Jonsen and Hellegers argue that to overcome these problems, it is necessary to avoid 'a facile appeal to the "inestimable social benefits of medicine" on the one hand, or to the "inviolable individual rights of patient or practitioner" on the other'.[12]

There is what amounts to a serious lacuna in medical ethics in the twentieth century. The health care industry is in all developed countries a major social service, with important (and varying) institutional arrangements where the quality and appropriateness of both health care and the institution are subject to political and public debate. Yet the medical profession holds to codes of ethics which do not adequately take this into account. Instead of recognising the hole, it would seem to want to attempt to paper it over with the other two doctrines of ethics: virtue and duty. Thus, we sometimes hear clinical freedom – part of an *individual* ethic – used to try to defend what could only be truly defensible on the basis of some ethic of the common good.

7.3 Why medical ethics?

The main reason for the existence of medical ethics lies in the nature of health care, as discussed in Chapter 3. In particular, in this context, the asymmetry of information and the knowledge of the asymmetry of information between doctor and patient are critical. For 'normal' goods and services – books, concerts, lawn-mowers – the individual is faced with a range of products about which he has various pieces of information concerning the utility he is likely to derive from them. Of course, it is not always the case that the expected utility/satisfaction (the basis of all consumer decisions) will equate with realised utility/satisfaction. (My avocado pear may turn out to be hard or rotten. But at least I will *know* when this occurs, and it will influence my future consumption pattern.)

But let us switch for a moment to even wider considerations. It can be argued that the philosophy of utilitarianism is the political basis of most Western democracies. But one of the apparent difficulties of utilitarianism is that it can be interpreted as being so much based on an individual ethic as to allow individuals (1) to do themselves harm and (2) to do so because of lack of appropriate information. The idea of maximising utility, the aim of utilitarianism and so dear to the hearts of many economists, has a very attractive ring to it – particularly when it is based on the idea of consumer sovereignty. Thus, the values underlying utilitarianism are usually seen as those of individuals.

As normally conceived, there are two aspects to utilitarianism: (1) individual, consumer sovereignty and (2) emphasis on utility being derived from what the individual receives. Given the nature of health care and what has been said about asymmetry of information, it would appear that we have a problem, should we wish to defend utilitarianism in medicine.

Harsanyi indicates that it is necessary 'to distinguish between a person's manifest preferences and his true preferences ... the latter being those ... he would have if he had all the relevant factual information, always reasoned with the greatest possible care and were in a state of mind most conductive to rational choice'.[13] The dangers of not adopting this stance are all too apparent; as Sen and Williams say, 'If people do not, in fact, get round to actually wanting what ... it would be rational for them to want, people may always be actually unsatisfied by the results of the correct policy.'[14]

Clearly, in health care there are very real problems for the individual in assessing his true preferences. It is this issue that is crucial to valuation in health care and, consequently, to the potential usefulness of utilitarianism in health care decision-making.

For the doctor to act to bridge the gap between the patient's manifest and true preferences (as disclosed in Chapter 6), it is not enough for him to consider what is prudent in *health* terms for his patient, were that patient fully informed. In pursuing what the doctor considers prudent, there will be some costs which will fall on the patient and which need to be assessed from the patient's point of view as if he (the patient) were perfectly prudent. What is the cost *to the patient* of his time off work or his loss of a game of golf – as judged by the doctor – assuming the patient were to act in a fully informed way? There will clearly also be costs to the doctor which will mean that this agency relationship will be at best 'incomplete' (see Evans[15]). Additionally there is plenty of evidence to indicate that doctors do not know best when assessing patients' quality of life.

There is a problem here which is important for medical ethics.

While we (as patients and potential patients) may be prepared to accept that 'the doctor knows best' when assessing health benefits, when it comes to weighing them against costs (of time, inconvenience, etc.) in the 'cost-benefit calculus' can we be as certain that he can estimate accurately such costs from the perspective of the 'perfectly prudent' patient? Following a discussion of the problems of cost estimation in cost-benefit analysis, Calabresi neatly encapsulates this issue as follows:[16]

> If the job of the physician, enforced through the code of ethics, is to maximise the patient's welfare, then that maximisation must involve the analogous valuation on his part of the costs to the patient of the alternative possible treatments. The physician is required by the code of ethics to balance the very same costs we have said were so hard to measure. We have not done away with the cost-benefit analysis for the costs and benefits are still the same, we only act as if they are not there by requiring the physician, through a code of ethics, to divine them. If he can't divine them adequately, then the code of ethics cannot work.

There is, however, a second difficulty here (raised initially in Chapter 5) and that is that utilitarianism is often based on the idea of utility being derived *solely* from what is obtained (i.e. 'outcome' utility). This is disputed by some utilitarians, particularly on the issue of the utility derived from freedom of choice. For example, Hahn suggests 'my utility may not only depend on what I (and others) get but on the manner in which I get it. That is why utility may not only depend on the consequences of policy but on the policy itself.'[17] The example he uses is as follows:

> Suppose that I give a certain amount to a particular charity. The government decides to tax me to that amount and gives it to the same charity. Am I indifferent between these two situations? Before the tax, I had the possibility of acting otherwise than I did even though I chose not to, after the tax the possibility is gone. But even if one attaches no probability of wishing to avail oneself of a possibility, its loss by restricting one's potential freedom may be felt as a loss of utility.

Here is a classic example of the utility of freedom of choice. Indeed, it is possible to take the view that even if the individual were to do himself harm and, after the event, know that he had done himself harm because he had acted on the basis of poor information, none the less he would have been resentful (suffered disutility?) if someone had interfered with his freedom of choice. For example, Mishan states that 'Person A may find himself disabled for life and rue his decision to take the risk. But this example is only a painful reminder of the fact that people come to regret a great many of the choices they make, notwithstanding which they would resent any interference with their future choices.'[18]

Fortunately, and sensibly, there is a middle ground – not born of the desire for compromise per se but rather perfectly rational – within the utilitarian goal of maximising utility. It can be argued that if people derive utility (positive *or* negative) from the process through which they receive a particular outcome, then that 'process' utility is relevant in deciding on how that person's overall utility is maximised. If this is the case (and it seems intuitively likely), it is clearly not enough to consider *outcome* utility alone.

Many have defended the concept of greater freedom of choice for consumers in health care. (For example, see Seldon.[19]) Indeed the reforms of the NHS are aimed at least in part at greater choice for patients. In the reforms this is in itself assumed to be 'a good thing'. But the decision on whether to opt for greater freedom of choice hinges not solely on the utility associated with that freedom (assuming it is positive) but also on the overall utility, including outcome utility, in the two situations of less (public) or more (private) freedom of choice. Given the very real problems (particularly of ignorance) for individuals in exercising choice in health care, freedom of choice may have a *negative* utility. Thus, process utility in health care which is of an NHS type may be positive, and individual freedom of choice may have an overall negative process utility.

For the present I want to suggest that medical ethics has a potential impact on utility in the context not only of *outcome* utility (i.e. that through the existence of an ethical code the consumer can be reassured that the doctor's recommendations for action can be equated with the way in which the patient would act were he perfectly prudent) but also of *process* utility (i.e. the nature of the delivery and organisation of health care). Thus, ethics, both individual ethics (virtue and duty) and collective ethics (the common good), will influence *how* the patient receives treatment. Indeed, the nature of the patient's demand for health care may well be in part a function of the nature and role of medical ethics in the health care system.

This comment on demand leads on to consideration of why *doctors* seek a medical ethic within which to operate. Zeckhauser puts forward three reasons.[20] He claims first that by adopting an ethical code the medical profession is able to create for itself 'a climate in which it is allowed to operate independent of the regulating procedures traditionally imposed on restricted-entry industries'. Second, he suggests that the *doctor* may gain reassurance from the existence of the code when he 'is facing difficult and delicate decisions. When he encounters a significantly unfortunate outcome ... the knowledge that he has acted in accordance with established ethical norms may make it far easier for him to accept the mischance.'

Finally, Zeckhauser argues that the introduction of ethics will shift the demand curve for medical care outwards (the quantity demanded of ethical care will be greater than that of 'unethical' care, all other things being equal). Thus, there may be pecuniary reasons for ethics where quantity demanded affects doctor remuneration. Essentially, therefore, there are both supply-side and demand-side arguments for medical ethics. To couch the issue in these 'market'-oriented terms may also be very appropriate since medical ethics, as distinct from health care ethics, is restricted largely to the individual ethics of virtue and duty. Jensen and Hellegers emphasise this point:[21]

> Just as the free market once consisted simply of a sole producer exchanging his produce for consideration by a single buyer ... so the medical transaction was, and still essentially is, a solo physician diagnosing and treating a single patient. But that essential transaction has gradually been surrounded by the indispensable cooperation of other people, by accessory producers, by physical environments, by customary and legal prescriptions.

The problem for the medical profession, and indeed all of us, is that medical ethics is the product of another time when medicine and the market had a much closer affinity. With the complexity of modern health care systems and the increased concern and involvement of governments in health services, the individualistic ethics of the medical profession need to be harnessed to (but not replaced by) an ethic of the common good. The 'invisible hand' of Adam Smith in the market-place of the eighteenth century may have been appropriate to medicine at that time.[22] It is much less so today.

Indeed, it is only the asymmetry of information between patient and doctor that has, to date, allowed the medical profession to continue to act as if the individualistic ethics of virtue and responsibility were enough.

7.4   Kennedy's critique of medical ethics

In the *Unmasking of Medicine* Kennedy writes in his Preface that he is concerned with 'power – the power of the professional, here the doctor', and he seeks to contrast this with 'the notion of the self-determination of the client, the patient, and his sense of responsibility for himself'.[23] Kennedy's other concerns included accountability, 'the need to ensure that the decisions of doctors, to the extent that they are not technical, conform to principles acceptable to all of us', and the fact that 'medicine is, at bottom, a political enterprise'.

Kennedy sought to provoke a debate about the nature of medicine in practice. Yet it seems that he missed his target or, to use his own analogy, that he removed the wrong part of the mask. Having outlined a programme to improve health he states that 'You may rest assured that those who would oppose it will find reasons of cost to justify doing so.'[24] He goes on 'I have little patience with such people. They hide their political choices behind slide rules and balance sheets.' Kennedy thus dismisses the issue of scarcity of resources, dealing with which must be one of the most important problems facing modern health care policy-makers. As suggested in Chapter 6, some doctors are undoubtedly romantics. Perhaps so too is Kennedy.

He maintains that 'good medical ethics' should embrace four principles omitted from current medical ethics: autonomy, dignity, justice and partnership. He places particular emphasis on justice, which he claims 'may call for consideration of people other than the particular patient; those, for example, who have less access to medical care, or have greater need of it, or those whose health suffers from a misallocation or maldistribution of resources'.[25]

It is worth emphasising that insofar as Kennedy departs from the cause of individualist ethics – and I can see considerable merit in his suggestion on that front – it is to consider justice or fairness. Indeed, he seeks to persuade doctors to become politically involved in the pursuit of justice. There is an inconsistency however in his argument, since he expresses unhappiness about the doctor's ability to determine on behalf of patients what doing good constitutes, thereby, according to Kennedy, undermining the patient's autonomy.

The fundamental issue here would seem to relate to the justified boundaries of medical power; that is, what are the property rights of doctors and what ought they to be? These are the questions which need to be answered and which Kennedy does not satisfactorily address. His main line of argument is not so much about the nature and extent of doctor power; rather, he considers that it is the value judgments they have that need to be corrected. One is left with the feeling that he would be happy if they had the same views as himself about what should be done to promote a healthy population.

The primary reason why medicine needs to be unmasked is not with respect to individual autonomy or dignity, nor partnership with the individual patient nor justice, at least not as Kennedy defines it. Rather, the key issue is that in aggregate, as societies, we have lost the right to determine the objectives and priorities for 'our' health care systems. The primacy of the freedom of the individual – particularly the individual doctor but also the individual patient – in health care has thwarted efforts at genuine social choice in health care. No government has been prepared to unmask the medical profession in the sense in which it matters; that is, to expose certain features (but by no means all) of their defence of current medical ethics and particularly clinical freedom as, in part, the usurping of democratic power in the name of doing good for the individual patient. In this the individual patient has inevitably been willing to play along since it is in his interest (selfishly) to do so.

Kennedy does not deal adequately with this issue. His stance is in essence elitist. He states: 'Our aim should be to create an environment more conducive to health for all, to the greatest extent possible, within the political framework, and conceding the necessity, indeed the desirability, of compromise.'[26]

This seems to be health for all, apparently irrespectively of whether people want it or not. This elitist stance is confirmed by his view of health education which he seems to see as a means of converting others to his cause, or at least his values. He states that health education 'is flawed in that it assumes that, once informed, the individual will change his behaviour or way of thinking'. The flaw arises essentially because many people disagree with Kennedy about the importance they attach to health. Why? According to Kennedy because 'the individual is, to a very large extent, the product of the social and political environment in which he finds himself; to the extent that knowing something does not necessarily mean that the individual will be able, or indeed sometimes want, to do anything about it'.

In raising these issues my point is a simple one. There *is* a problem in medicine. Kennedy has, to throw his own phrase back at him, 'swatted the symptoms'; but he has got the diagnosis wrong. The answer is not for the medical profession to endorse Kennedy's value judgments; it is for society in aggregate to be better able to control and influence the objectives, directions and priorities of health care than it currently is and thereby exercise greater control and influence over the medical profession much more than it currently does.

As a member of society and as a potential patient I have three fundamental interests in health care: first, having good health care available to me and everyone else in this society; second, ensuring that somebody, somewhere, keeps some check on the supply side of health care, since as an individual I cannot; and third, insisting that the share of the nation's resources going on health care is reasonable, given all the other desirable things in my life. As a society can we not recognise that a lot of the potential for attaining these goals rests in our own collective hands?

The reforms of the NHS are discussed in some detail in Chapter 10. However, in the context of some of the points made here on ethics and the role of societies in influencing health care objectives and priorities, it is possible to see the reforms as a backward step. Whatever the other merits might be of the reforms of the NHS – and I think there are several – their emphasis on the individual, the ideas of freedom of choice and of the virtues of choice may well be at best overstated, at worst misplaced.

There is a model of health care which emphasises the power of the market in the pursuit of efficiency. Whatever one's interpretation of the success of that model, there is no doubt that its roots lie in the ideas of the private market and the efficiency with which private markets act. Private markets can promote efficiency but they require that several assumptions are fulfilled before this efficiency goal can be achieved. Not least among these is the need to have fully informed consumers. That is not the case in health care. This is not to argue that consumer preferences are always inappropriate in health care but there has to be some concern about the extent to which there are many occasions when the patient and the potential patient are well placed to exercise rational preferences. There are arguments for trying to get doctors to provide attractive waiting rooms, to be nice to their patients and to take account of the time costs to patients of waiting in their surgeries. Provided that patients want and demand, i.e. are willing to pay (and sufficiently) for, such 'process' considerations, then there are good arguments for providing these features efficiently in health care.

But it is pertinent to ask: can such mechanisms work with the delivery of health? Can we as patients recognise a good doctor? Indeed can we distinguish a good doctor from a nice doctor?

The NHS reforms are a long way from the private market and there can be little doubt that the NHS was suffering from certain forms of inefficiency prior to the reforms. There was a case for taking a radical look at what had become a quite worryingly conservative organisation. But on certain scores − and the push for individualism and 'consumerism' in the new NHS is one − this looks like a mistaken view of how to create efficiency in health care.

At the time of writing it seems that patients' freedom of choice is being reduced along some dimensions at least − and ones that appear to matter to the patients such as equality of access. But did patients really want greater choice in changing their GPs?

A more fundamental and general question can be asked. Do patients in principle want more freedom of choice? While the answer may be yes, there is a need to address this question rather than simply assume (as appears the case in the UK and seemingly more and more in other countries, e.g. Denmark) that more patient choice is itself 'a good thing'. (This is discussed in the context of the NHS reforms in Chapter 10.)

These issues again involve certain ethical considerations about the social choices involved in health care. They are difficult ones to disentangle. There are few absolute 'rights' and 'wrongs' here but there are possibilities for better and worse solutions. In this respect on the reforms I think that the position may well be worse. What is needed here is not dogma but a genuine attempt to find out two things (which I do not think would prove so difficult): what do patients want from their doctors? And what do citizens want from their health services? Perhaps such an exercise would reveal that patients and citizens do want more freedom of choice and in that respect I would then be proved wrong. More importantly than whether I am right or wrong, however, is that the question be put rather than the answer assumed.

7.5   The relevance of utilitarianism

Veatch examines a hypothetical island where pursuit of the concept of utilitarianism (which is clearly one way of defining the common good, and one frequently favoured by economists in cost-benefit analyses) appeared to create certain problems.[27] Given the task of identifying the best health care programme (i.e. the one which provided the greatest net benefit to the island), the planners discovered that the best buy 'would simultaneously reduce mortality rates, morbidity rates, infant mortality and other indicators of health problems ... and it would not be ... expensive ... or difficult to administer'.

However, this particular programme 'would require social scientists to identify the 1 per cent of the population that was chronically ill with incurable illness, possessing insufficient intelligence to follow a medical regimen and receiving expensive medical care. Excluding this population, which would be banned from receiving any further health care, a universal health maintenance system would be established for the island.'

The issue was then: should the island's government implement the programme? It is a thought-provoking and useful example, but I find it difficult to accept Veatch's statement that in such situations 'we are trapped between the ultraindividualism of the Hippocratic medical ethic and the social indiscrimination of utilitarians'.

Let us simplify his example. There is available on the island a very limited quantity of drug X. This has two unique properties. It can alleviate the pain of a group of fifty patients or it can save the lives of another group of a hundred patients. Without it, the first group will exist in pain rather than without pain; the second group will die rather than live.

Set in these terms, not to relieve the pain of the first group may well be the best bet in terms of the net benefit to society at large. However, it need not be. If it is a caring society, then it is quite possible that the greatest net benefit will be provided by a programme which reduces the pain a little for the fifty at the expense of one death among the hundred who might have been saved. Indeed, this could be one explanation for resorting to the rule utility that Veatch suggests; that is, 'The interests of society could be allowed to surface only in the formulation of principles or rules that would produce the greatest good in the long run'.[28]

That, however, seems not to be quite the point. Rather, it may be that what Veatch includes in his definition of utility is inadequate. While not explicit about this, it appears that he includes only the outcome utility in terms of health status changes. However, as mentioned briefly in the previous section and as we will discuss in more detail in Chapter 9, the notion of 'process utility' may also be relevant. If this is the case, then in addition to each individual islander's valuations of his own health status we may have to add to the calculus:

1. The valuation of each islander of the health status of all *other* islanders (which might in many cases be zero but in some at least would be positive); in other words, a measure of caring for others (see Chapter 9).
2. The valuation of the islanders of the health care institution; that is their valuations of health care may not be independent of the process involved in obtaining health care.

Build these in and utilitarianism seems to take on a new lease of life. For example, at one point Veatch argues that 'One of the problems of the utilitarian ethical principle is that, at least hypothetically, it seems to justify too much. It would have justified the Nazi experiments if only the Nazis had been clever enough to devise experiments that really produced benefit on balance.'[29] This is a most peculiar comment. Given the enormous cost in all sorts of dimensions and the lack of or extremely limited benefit of the experiments the Nazis did conduct, it certainly doesn't seem likely that 'the utilitarian ethical principle' could be used to justify them at all. If they 'had been clever enough to devise experiments that really produced benefit on balance', then presumably the atrocities would not have occurred. There is some confused thinking here on Veatch's part. Certainly for my part I can only wish in this particular context that the Nazis had been utilitarians able with perfect foresight to weight up the costs and benefits of their actions.

Other criticisms of utilitarianism arise from those who believe that it plays down the issue of individual autonomy and the concept of duty. Much of this criticism is Kantian in origin.[30] This is summed up by Fried as follows:[31]

> The touchstone of everything we care about, the touchstone of value is persons – free persons, moral persons. They are the source of value. And what is it about persons which makes them the source of value? The Kantian answer ... is the capacity of persons to reflect, to reach judgments, to make judgments both about truth and falsehood but also about what their lives should be, what value consists of, what will be their good, how they shall live their lives ... So the capacity for reflection, for judgment, and then the capacity for choice, the capacity to act upon the conclusions of those reflections are what make for the worth of moral beings.

It is this emphasis in Kant on 'the capacity for reflection, for judgment' followed by 'the capacity for choice' that is the basis of much criticism of utilitarianism. This is summarised by Glover who suggests that utilitarianism can be attacked on 'moral objections, based on appeals to other, non-utilitarian, values. It is said that, for the utilitarian, "the end justifies the means", and that the means may include morally objectionable acts of dishonesty, injustice, cruelty or killing.'[32]

The difficulties here in the context of health care are essentially two. First, and as was discussed in detail in Chapters 3 and 5, the extent to which the individual is capable of reflection and judgment and has 'the capacity for choice', in the context of his choices for his health care, is limited. It is not even limited uniformly, being greater in primary care than in acute hospital care. Second, even if the individual does have the capacity or is given the capacity (and that is unlikely to be a costless exercise), it may well be that he simply does not want to do the choosing.

Clearly, there will be occasions where these competing philosophies will come into conflict. What is essential is that medical ethics in practice should accept more than it currently does that there is an important role for utilitarianism in health care valuation and, consequently, for the ethics of the common good. (The debate on this issue is picked up again i' Chapter 10.)

7.6   Conclusion

This chapter has attempted to highlight the source of the friction
between economics and medicine: essentially, social versus individualistic ethical bases coming into conflict. There may be those
who would argue that making this conflict explicit is a mistake and
that it is better to accept that doctors will pursue (and legitimately)
clinical ends and that it has to be (legitimately) left to others to
resolve the social and economic issues. In a sense I agree – if it were
happening in that way. It is by no means clear that it is.

This takes us back to the agency relationship as discussed in
Chapter 6. There it was suggested that the doctor–patient relationship could be seen in the context of the doctor acting on behalf of
the poorly informed patient. And that would seem to be what much
of medicine is about. With that I have no complaint. What would
seem inappropriate is for the individual doctor to be in a position
to affect the priorities for health care in the sense of their values
being used in determining or influencing the allocation of resources
between for example the old and the young, psychiatric care and
maternity care, etc.

The case for making explicit this conflict between the social and
the individual has been put by Harman in the context of the rich
and powerful on the one hand and the poor and weak on the
other.[33]

> Those who are not rich and powerful have not failed to notice the
> self-interested motives that can lead the rich and powerful to appeal
> to liberty and property rights. The rich and powerful have in turn
> not failed to notice the self-interested motives that can lead the poor
> and weak to emphasize equality. Each side is conscious of the
> self-interested reasons the other side has, while being perhaps less
> conscious of the way in which they themselves are motivated by
> self-interest.
>
> There are advantages to making such self-interested motives
> explicit. Doing so would lead to greater clarity and honesty and less
> hypocrisy in moral argument. This would further values that are
> already part of our morality. It would also tend to diminish
> pointless taboos and superstitions. And that might reduce certain
> sorts of exploitation.

Clearly, it is to be hoped and expected that when we move this
analogy to the doctor and patient then a major part of the doctor's

concern will be for his patient and not for himself. But there have to be occasions when a conflict will arise at the level of doctor/patient or doctor (patient-interest)/doctor (self-interest). An understanding of the motives involved and their strengths would seem to provide a focus for trying to ensure that the patient's manifest preferences do as often as possible and as far as possible end up as his true preferences. And the best way to achieve that is to make the terms of this conflict explicit.

The analogy with Harman's rich and powerful versus the poor and weak raises explicitly the question of power. There has to be concern on the part of the individual that no matter the extent to which the doctor operates out of patient-interest, there remains the need for reassurance that this will always be the case and that the risk of exploitation by the informed supplier is minimised, as previously discussed in the context of the agency relationship in Chapter 6.

It would seem likely, however, that the risk of exploitation and the extent to which any level of such risk is seen as problematical will vary from country to country or perhaps from health care system to health care system. As Harman states, and as is debated at greater length in Chapter 9, 'people differ in the extent to which they value individuality and freedom as compared with community spirit and a harmonious society. And this affects the way in which they evaluate their own and other social systems'.[34] It can also be readily argued that attitudes to individuality are not constant over time. Indeed it is possible that it is changed values at this level that are being reflected in the reforms of the NHS.

Notes

1. G. Mooney and A. McGuire, *Medical Ethics and Economics in Health Care* (Oxford University Press: Oxford, 1988).
2. I. Kennedy, *The Unmasking of Medicine* (Paladin: London, 1983).
3. J.A. Muir Gray, 'Choosing priorities', *Journal of Medical Ethics*, 5 (1979), pp 73, 74.
4. G.H. Mooney, 'Cost-benefit analysis and medical ethics', *Journal of Medical Ethics*, 6 (1980), p 178.
5. A.R. Jonsen and A.E. Hellegers, 'Conceptual foundations for an ethics of medical care' in *Ethics of Health Care*, ed. L.R. Tancredi (National Academy of Sciences: Washington, DC, 1987), p 4.

6. R.M. Veatch, *A Theory of Medical Ethics* (Basic Books: New York, 1980), p 17.
7. Jonsen and Hellegers, *op. cit.*, p 5.
8. British Medical Association, *The Handbook of Medical Ethics* (BMA: London, 1984), p 67.
9. Jonsen and Hellegers, *op. cit.*, p 12.
10. Veatch, *op. cit.*, p 170.
11. Jonsen and Hellegers, *op. cit.*, p 13.
12. *Ibid.*, p 18.
13. J.C. Harsanyi, 'Morality and the theory of rational behaviour' in *Utilitarianism and Beyond*, eds. A. Sen and B. Williams (Cambridge University Press: Cambridge, 1982), p 55.
14. A. Sen and B. Williams, 'Introduction', in *ibid.*, p 10.
15. R.G. Evans, *Strained Mercy* (Butterworth: Toronto, 1984).
16. G. Calabresi, commentary on Arrow, in Tancredi, ed., *op. cit.* p 51.
17. F. Hahn, 'On some difficulties of the utilitarian economist', in Sen and Williams, eds, *op. cit.*, pp 188, 189.
18. E.J. Mishan, *Cost-Benefit Analysis* (George Allen and Unwin: London, 1971), p 318.
19. A. Seldon, ed., *The Litmus Papers, A National Health Dis-Service* (Centre for Policy Studies: London, 1980).
20. R.J. Zeckhauser, commentary, in Tancredi, ed., *op. cit.*, p 90.
21. Jonsen and Hellegers, *op. cit.*, p 14.
22. A. Smith, *The Wealth of Nations* (The Grand Colosseum Warehouse: Glasgow, 1869; first published 1776).
23. Kennedy, *op. cit.*, p ix.
24. *Ibid.*, p 79.
25. *Ibid.*, p 123.
26. *Ibid.*, p 64.
27. Veatch, *op. cit.*, pp 172–5.
28. *Ibid.*, p 175.
29. *Ibid.*, p 174.
30. I. Kant, *The Critique of Pure Reason* (Macmillan: New York and London, 1934).
31. C. Fried, 'Distributive justice', *Social Philosophy and Policy*, 1 (1984), p 50.
32. J. Glover, *Causing Death and Saving Lives*, (Penguin: Harmondsworth, 1977).
33. G. Harman, 'Justice and moral bargaining', *Social Philosophy and Policy*, 1 (1984), p 128.
34. *Ibid.*, p 116.

8

Just health care: only medicine?

Mirror, mirror on the wall,
What is the fairest of them all?

8.1   Introduction

Whatever the financing mechanism, the question of justice and equity in health care seems important. Whatever else people dispute in health service policy, there is general agreement that fairness should be a part of health care. The question of why this is so is left to Chapter 9. The answers to the questions of what fairness is, or should be, and the weight to be attached to it are much less than immediately apparent.

What is discussed in this chapter initially is the confusion surrounding equity in health care; I do not want to attempt to resolve the problem, just to point to the need for clarity in setting the goals of equity. Thereafter some of the practical difficulties involved in pursuing equity are debated before highlighting some of the implications, particularly for other objectives such as efficiency, in choosing one equity objective rather than another. Finally, the chapter returns to issues of ethics, but specifically those related to equity. What emerges is that ethics and equity are interdependent, as are ethics and efficiency and, in turn, equity and efficiency. Perhaps that is inevitable. The explicit recognition of it, however, seems far from inevitable, particularly among the medical profession. There would appear to be a case for trying to change that.

8.2   What is equity?

In an attempt to highlight the definitional problems, I have elsewhere suggested seven possible definitions of equity.[1] Readers will no doubt be able to think of others. The list is as follows. Equality of:

1. Expenditure per capita.
2. Inputs per capita.
3. Inputs for equal need.
4. Access for equal need.
5. Utilisation for equal need.
6. Marginal met need.
7. Health.

There are practical problems in attempting to implement most of these notions of equity. But prior to discussing that issue it is relevant to explain some of these definitions. The distinction between 1 and 2 is simply that, as between two different areas of a country, prices of the relevant manpower, goods and services which comprise the inputs into health care may differ. As a result, a fixed level

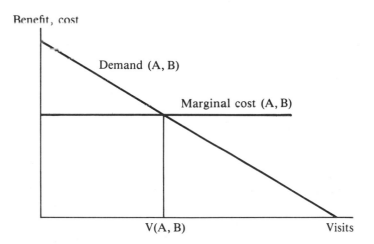

Figure 8.1   Equal access, equal demand

of expenditure may buy more inputs in one location that in another.

The distinction between access (as in 4) and utilisation (as in 5) is that the former is wholly a supply-side phenomenon and the latter is a function of both supply and demand (or need). In other words, equal access means that two (or more) individuals face the same costs to themselves of using the health care facility (e.g. as a proxy it might be that they live the same distance from the facility). Whether they use it equally will be dependent on their valuation of that use; in other words, their demand for health and health care. Various aspects of this can be shown diagrammatically, for visits to a general practitioner. From these figures we can see that if two individuals face equal costs of access and have equal demands for health care, utilisation of health care will also be the same. If they have different access but equal demands, they will have different utilisation. If they have both different access and different demand, it is likely but not necessarily the case that their utilisation will differ. (Thus, in Figure 8.4, if the marginal cost curve for B had been a little higher, V(A) and V(B) would have been the same.)

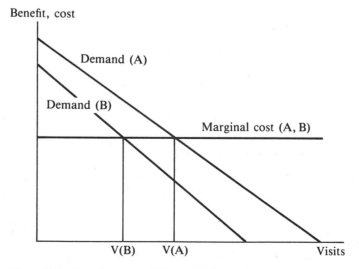

Figure 8.2 Equal access, differential demand

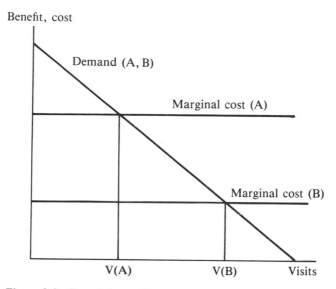

Figure 8.3 Equal demand, differential access

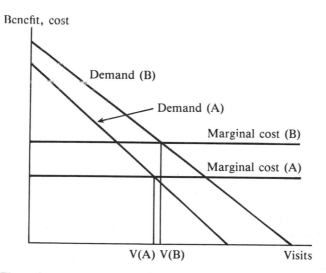

Figure 8.4 Differential demand, differential access

These distinctions seem simple enough. Yet both Aday, Anderson and Fleming[2] and, again, Daniels,[3] who have written at length on equity in health care, tend to confuse access and utilisation. There is no need for such confusion.

Equality of marginal met need (definition 6 above) may warrant a little more explanation. It is based on the cost-benefit approach and was developed by Steele.[4] *Ceteris paribus*, a rational health authority, operating under a budget constraint, will allocate its scarce resources to those activities for which the ratios of benefit to costs are highest. It will continue to do this until it has used up its total allocation or expenditure. It will therefore want to establish ranking of needs to be met, the ranking being based on the size of the benefit/cost ratio involved in tackling different needs.

Adopting this process does not necessarily mean that something like heart transplants or kidney dialysis would be ranked highly. While success in these areas certainly would bring with it high benefits, it also brings high costs, and success may be far from certain. Consequently, it could be that high ranking will be associated with relatively low benefit programmes — if they happen to be low cost as well.

Diagrammatically, if we were concerned with equity regionally in a country, the picture we would get for equating marginal met need in two different regions would be as in Figure 8.5.

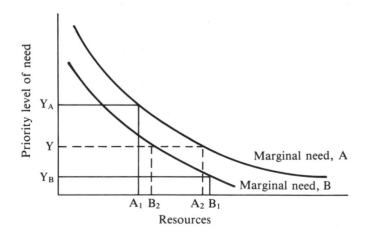

Figure 8.5 Marginal met need

Let us assume that initially the resources available in region A are A_1 and in region B, B_1. The needs just met are Y_A in A and Y_B in B. To equate marginal met need requires a redistribution of the total resources available $(A_1 + B_1)$ until both regions are meeting the same marginal need. This occurs at A_2 and B_2 (note that $A_2 + B_2$ must equal $A_1 + B_1$) when the marginal met need is the same (i.e. Y).

8.3 Practical difficulties

Problems in practice will vary depending on what definition is chosen. However, they all relate to measurement, primarily of need but also of the groups across which we want to be equitable. (For example, there are problems in defining social classes.) In order to highlight these difficulties and at the same time to discuss the practicalities of getting to grips with the equity issue, this section outlines, first, the way that the UK government has attempted to foster regional equity, and second, an analysis of the extent to which social class inequalities exist and can be measured.

While the emphasis placed on the objective of equity in health care inevitably varies from one country to another, many of the problems in this area are common. Consequently, while the example here is drawn from the UK, it has wider relevance. Indeed, the publication of the UK report on geographical equity in health care appeared to spark off an international industry in the 1970s and 1980s in regional resource allocation formulas. Whether that continues in the 1990s we must wait and see.

The first example, drawn from the Report of the Resource Allocation Working Party (RAWP)[5] indicates how, against a background of concern that the original equity objectives of the NHS were not being met, a formula was devised to try to distribute equitably the central funds available for the NHS to the various regional health authorities responsible for running the health service. It represented an attempt at allocating funds according to need – purportedly on an access definition of equity (i.e. definition 4 above).

As a result of the reform of the NHS, RAWP may be dead in the form that it is set out here. However, at the time of writing there remains some doubt about precisely what the basis will be on which the UK government will in future allocate NHS resources to the regions. As Carr-Hill[6] indicates, there is some disagreement in the government papers published on this topic. (See for example Department of Health 1989,[7] para. 4.8 and Department of Health, 1989a[8]). Further, Carr-Hill[9] points out that 'the conceptual difference between the new allocation mechanism and the original RAWP formula may be more apparent than real'.

Whatever happens, the RAWP formula is a good example of an attempt to put equitable distribution of health care resources, in this case geographically, into a formula. As such, whether RAWP survives the reforms of the NHS is secondary. There are still good lessons to be learnt from it.

RAWP was the official response of the UK government to the question of whether it is fair or equitable for an individual to be penalised in his access to health care simply because of what part of the country he happens to live in – London, Yorkshire or East Anglia. Or again, is there any reason why one region of the country should receive more per capita by way of resources than another region?

With regard to the relevant organisational features of the NHS, all that is necessary to know is that:

1. The NHS is funded very largely through central government taxes and is mainly zero money priced at the point of consumption.
2. For all services (except family practitioner services, i.e. general practitioners, general dentists and general ophthalmologists who are independent contractors but paid directly by central government), the government has to divide the total budget available between the fourteen regional health authorities who have responsibility for administering the services in each region.
3. RAWP was about how to divide that cake up equitably.

The methods used prior to RAWP to distribute financial resources from the centre to the regions were largely supply orientated. In other words, they were heavily influenced by what facilities happened to exist and therefore happened to be taken over by the NHS when it was established in 1948.

The stated objective of RAWP was couched in terms of equal

opportunity of access for those at equal risk. It should also be stressed that RAWP was concerned with need, not supply or demand. Consequently, the approach adopted was aimed at measuring relative need for health care in different regions and then allocating expenditures *pro rata* with these estimates of relative needs.

The factors deemed relevant to estimates of relative need were as follows:

1. Size of population − the simple basis that health care is for people. In passing, it is worth noting that population size is always likely to prove the biggest factor in determining relative need for health care for different groups in society.
2. Composition − the elderly and the young tend to have greater need for health care than those in the middle age range. Also, women have different needs than men (although here only those affecting health care are relevant). Consequently, the age/sex composition of the population will affect estimates of relative need.
3. Morbidity − the more sick a population is, *ceteris paribus*, the greater is its need for health care.
4. Cost − some conditions may prove more expensive to treat than others so the *nature* of morbidity may be relevant. Again, the cost of providing facilities may vary between regions; for example, salary levels for the same grades of staff may vary or economies of scale may not be capable of being reaped as readily in sparsely populated rural areas as in dense urban areas.
5. Patient cross-boundary flows − there may be patient flows into or out of various regions.
6. Medical education − this is not spread equally across the different regions and some allowance will need to be made for this.
7. Capital investment − while capital allocations for new building, and so on, will be influenced by the factors as in 1 to 6 above, it may also be necessary to adjust for not only quantitative differences in capital stock but also differences in qualitative factors such as age.

One of the difficulties in pursuing a formula incorporating all these factors in estimating relative regional needs is that the needs for all these services cannot all be assumed to be influenced to the same extent by them. Another is that the information required to estimate them is not always available, at least not in an ideal form.

To overcome the former problem, the services provided by the NHS were disaggregated into seven different categories as follows. (The figures in brackets are the estimated national percentages of revenue expenditure on each service.)

1. Non-psychiatric inpatient services   (55.9)
2. All day and outpatient services   (13.4)
3. Mental illness inpatient services   (8.8)
4. Mental handicap inpatient services   (3.5)
5. Community services   (12.2)
6. Ambulance services   (5.7)
7. Administration of family practitioner services   (0.5)

                                           Total   (100.0)

The relative need was calculated in each region for each of these services. This was weighted by the relevant percentage figure above, and then all seven figures for each region were summed to give the overall regional weight. (This was then further adjusted to allow for cross-boundary flows and teaching.)

The procedure was similar for each of the seven listed services, although the weighting factors sometimes varied (e.g. marital status was included as a relevant influence on the relative need for mental illness inpatient services). For non-psychiatric hospital inpatient services, for example, the report recommended that the population should be weighted for age and sex according to national bed utilisation for each condition and then adjusted to take account of condition-specific Standardised Mortality Ratios (SMRs) for each region. (SMRs are discussed below.)

What does this mean in practice? It means, first, estimating the population size − say, 5 million people − then saying that if the people in that area tend to be rather old and, in addition, that even allowing for their age they are rather more sick (this is the 'SMR' above of which more below) than the average nationally, then they should get an extra allowance in funding (at the expense of a younger, healthier region). The extent of this increase in this context should be determined by national bed utilisation rates for different conditions. If age and sickness mean that this region's health needs are 10 per cent above the average, then the 'notional' population becomes not 5 million but 5.5 million. Thus, assuming a total England population of 50 million, the proportion of the budget available for non-psychiatric inpatient services going to this region should be not 10 per cent (i.e. 5 in 50 million) but 11 per cent (i.e. 5.5 in 50 million). Since that budget is 55.9 per cent of the overall NHS budget, the need for non-psychiatric inpatient services in this region suggests that 11 per cent of 55.9 per cent of the total budget should be allocated to this region for these services (i.e. 6.15 per cent). To this would then be added the allocation for the other six services. The cross-boundary flow and teaching adjustments would follow on.

While there is a great deal of logic to this approach, there are weaknesses in it, largely related to lack of appropriate information. These are basically that:

1. It assumes that relative total need is a meaningful concept (doubtful given the discussion in Chapter 6).
2. It assumes that relative total need can be measured sufficiently accurately by relatively few factors.
3. The measurement of relative morbidity used is suspect (again, readers will be ready to understand the difficulties here given the discussion on output measurement in Chapter 4).

To some extent these problems can be overcome by adopting the 'marginal met need' approach suggested by Steele (see above). However, in the context of RAWP the first problem was ignored and the second, which probably does not lead to major inaccuracies in practice, side stepped.

On the third point, the measure of morbidity used was the SMR (Standardised Mortality Ratio). This statistic compares the number of deaths actually occurring in a region with those that would be expected if the national mortality ratios by age and sex were applicable to the population of that region. The reason for using this statistic as a measure of relative morbidity is simply that there is no good and reliable measure of relative morbidity available regionally in the UK.

Once the calculations had been completed and the report published, it created a political uproar, largely because it resulted in a redistribution away from the affluent south-east and London to the rest of the country. However, the recommendations of the report were gradually implemented, and while there are undoubtedly flaws in the formula adopted, few would disagree that it has resulted in a more equitable distribution of health care resources than was the case previously. Indeed its very success is part of the reason why it may be abandoned. It is suggested that RAWP has done its job.

Interestingly, in the context of the discussion on defining equity above, despite the report's claims to be concerned with an objective of access, it did not in practice succeed in getting beyond equality of input for equal need.

The extent to which the RAWP formula has been subject to debate in the UK (and beyond) makes it a particularly interesting example of an attempt to put health care equity into a mathematical formula. (For one interesting account of the debate see Carr-Hill.[10])

Here I want to look at just one aspect of this. There was some feeling at the time of RAWP that there was inadequate account taken of 'deprivation' and that in this respect the formula was deficient. As a result, Jarman[11] developed some indices of deprivation. I do not want to discuss these in detail but rather point to one possible problem here that I think is worth highlighting.

In the RAWP formula, as indicated above, attempts are made to take account of relative need through proxies for morbidity (which are in fact related to mortality). Insofar as these succeed (and we can obviously question that) then why do we need a deprivation index additionally? Certainly there is good evidence that the poor tend to be ill more than the rich and presumably the deprived even more so than the poor (if we can differentiate between these categories). So there is a very real risk of double counting in introducing deprivation.

However, there may be another reason for considering deprivation (although this appears not to have been the explanation for the 'Jarman index'). It might represent an attempt to move towards some more genuine concept of equality of access. In other words, if equality of inputs for equal need were established, for the 'deprived' there might still be poorer access than for the non-deprived since they might be less well aware of the availability of services or perhaps less able to use them for various reasons. Then a 'deprivation index' might help to overcome these access problems.

In a more general sense, however, the question of the appropriateness of using some deprivation index in this way would hinge on two issues. First, is access the dimension in which the goal of equity is to be stated (which takes us back to the debate at the early part of this chapter)? And second, how are deprivation and access related? This second issue would seem to be a rather important but at the same time very difficult one to assess. (Some interesting Australian work suggests that there the introduction of Medicare for all meant that about 15 per cent of the population who had previously had no insurance became eligible for health insurance, i.e. had their access to health care improved. These certainly were largely if not totally people who would fit the description of the 'deprived'. However Hall[12] in following these individuals and their health status through time, could find no evidence of an improvement in their health status as a result of improved access.)

That raises the interesting question of how equity affects the financing of health care, an issue dealt with at some length in the next chapter.

8.4   How should equity be defined?

There is no uniquely correct way of defining equity. It is dependent on a value judgment both about equity per se and about the relative weights to be attached to it *vis-à-vis* other objectives of any health care system. One aspect of this that requires close examination is the potential trade-off between equity and efficiency.

By way of example, let us assume that the definition of equity we are using is 'equality of access for equal needs' (see page 103). Assume too that the country we are considering is composed of one large island with a population of 490,000 and five small islands each with a population of 2,000. There is a major teaching hospital on the main island, the small islands are served locally solely by general practitioners. In such circumstances, whatever the overall level of spending on health care, it seems inevitable that equal access to high quality inpatient hospital care can only be bought at a high price. And if we assume that the budget is fixed, then that price must be in terms of health care facilities, and we can assume health. Consequently, there can be a trade-off between equity and efficiency. Thus, maximising health may not be achievable from a given budget where another objective relates to equity.

This trade-off, however, will not always be present. Where the issue is one of dealing equally with equals (what has been called by West 'horizontal equity'[13]) then equity and efficiency will tend to move together. However, in vertical equity – the unequal treatment of unequals – there is likely to be a conflict with efficiency. For example, in the context of prevention, it may be that reducing risks by a little for the majority of the population will save fewer lives than concentrating the same resources on the few at high risk. An added difficulty with vertical equity is determining the degree of inequality which exists and deciding the extent to which that justifies or merits treatment inequalities. Clearly, the problems of output measurement, discussed in detail in Chapter 4, arise here with a vengeance. It is in this context of vertical equity that de Jong and Rutten write that the 'basic practical problem facing an egalitarian policy is ... how to decide which patients are the worst-off and should therefore receive priority ... such a comparison requires', as they go on to say so appositely, 'an aggregate measure of expected misery'.[14]

Broadly, as we move through the definitions of equity from 1 to 7 listed earlier in this chapter (page 103), so it will tend to be the case that the trade-off with efficiency will increase. (Definition 6, relating to marginal met need, does not fit this trend.) If, for example, given all the other influences on health outside the health service, the choice of the definition of equity should be equality of health, presumably age standardised, insofar as this is at all feasible, it could only be at a very low level of health. In other words, equal health would mean equally bad health.

Consequently, in any decision on what the equity goal is to be, it is important to attempt to assess the impact of that choice on other health service goals. It is not enough to want to pursue an efficient, equitable health care policy. Questions have to be posed about *how* efficient and *how* equitable.

For economists there is a lot of appeal, in principle at least, in the marginal met need approach as proposed by Steele.[15] It avoids the problems thrown up by RAWP of attempting to measure relative total need in different regions and concentrates firmly on where economists love to be: on the margin. Whether it is feasible in practice depends on a number of issues. First, it requires that different regions can rank needs in priority for being met. Second, it is necessary that regions have the same ranking. Third, it ideally requires that all regions are efficient or at least equally inefficient. (On this last point, if it is the case that one region is not getting as far down its marginal need curve as another, it may be because it is not so much 'short' of resources as just not being as efficient.) It is this last point that is most problematical because the process could lead to an encouragement of inefficiency which would certainly not be welcomed by economists. In other words, it would create perverse incentives. Yet, at the same time, to me it is in some way inequitable that under a RAWP-type system no allowance is made for the fact that, let us say, I live in a part of the country with the least efficient health authority.

On the basis of informal questioning of colleagues and students, in practice it appears that faced with the choice between the seven definitions presented above, most opt for a mix of equal inputs for equal need and equal access for equal need, the mix to be determined empirically by examining the trade-off between access and health. I would support that view if equating marginal met need cannot be made a practical alternative.

Equality of utilisation is, in my view, too elitist. I cannot accept the notion of compulsory health care: 'You will use the health service just like the sensible middle classes.' Equality of health is simply too expensive, in terms of sacrifices to health and other good things in this life.

8.5 Equity and ethics

There are many who would argue that equity in health care is a matter of ethics, an issue already touched on in Chapter 7. For example, Kennedy suggests that 'the most important ... basic moral principle' is that of 'seeking to do justice or equity among people ... the omission of which from the ambit of current medical ethics I regard as the most serious'.[16] It is *this* aspect that concerns Kennedy on the question of the emphasis on the individual in current medical ethics, not the efficiency issue I discussed in Chapter 7.

He states that: 'If acting justly, doing justice, were seen to be *the* fundamental moral principle, good medical ethics would clearly mean abandonment of the Hippocratic tradition.' Thus, Kennedy places equity lexicographically above all other principles and seems unaware that the pursuit of equity can result in less health than might otherwise be the case.

Veatch, in the context of medical ethics, discusses four theories of justice.[17] The first of these – entitlement theory – suggests we are all entitled to what we have, provided we have acquired it justly. The well-to-do have no obligation to help the less-well-to-do; the distribution of entitlements is essentially a matter of luck, and the lucky have no duty to look after the unfortunates. It is in effect an amoral theory of justice. However, as soon as one concedes that some existing distribution of resources is less than fair – surely especially true of the distribution of health – the theory would seem to fall apart.

Utilitarianism, Veatch's second theory of justice, has already been discussed in detail in Chapter 7. He states that the approach of 'serving the greatest good for the greatest number ... is a favourite strategy of health planners and economists'.[18] But utilitarianism is not really a theory of justice. Indeed, one of the criticisms made of it is that it is devoid of an ethics of justice. It is essentially about efficiency, not equity.

Veatch then looks at the maximin theory, best exemplified in Rawls' theory of justice,[19] and which relates very much to the idea that there is some duty or simply wish that the worst off be given high priority. If people operating behind a veil of ignorance such that they do not know their position in society were asked what sort of society they wished, Rawls suggests they would opt for one of maximising benefit to the least well off. Such a proposal says nothing about the costs to the rest of society in pursuing such a policy – a rather important consideration in a world not hiding behind a veil of ignorance.

Finally Veatch's fourth theory of justice is the theory of egality, that is essentially, 'equality of net welfare for individuals'.[20] For this, in the context of health care, equality of health would be the goal.

What is important for our discussion is to note that these ethical overtones are present in much of this discussion, at least in two of these theories, maximin and egalitarianism. It is studiously omitted from the entitlement theory and played down and perhaps even missing from the utilitarian theory. More discussion of these issues in Chapter 9 will, I think, reveal that there are considerable advantages in accepting what is essentially a utilitarian non-ethical view of justice and one which avoids the problems of imposing an unwanted (and hence one bearing negative utility) code of justice on the society concerned.

But what of equity in the context of the medical profession? Is there a justice that they do or should subscribe to? As indicated previously in Chapter 7, the British Medical Association's *Handbook of Medical Ethics* states that 'as the resources available within the NHS are limited, the doctor has a general duty to advise on their equitable allocation and efficient utilisation'.[21] It is important to note that what the doctor is to do with respect to equity and efficiency in order to act ethically is to *advise*, not to be. Equally important, even this advisory role is to be 'subordinate to his professional duty to the individual who seeks his clinical advice'.

Also relevant to our discussion is the section in the BMA *Handbook* entitled 'The Doctor as an Impartial Expert',[22] which is separate from the section dealing with 'The Doctor in Personal Medical Care', an interesting separation in itself. Under the former, when community medicine is discussed we find that community physicians 'face ethical problems of a different nature' − presumably different from non-community physicians − one of which is 'those affecting the individual patient and the community'. The implication is thus that the clinician, beyond *advising* on equity and efficiency, has not the responsibility which the community medicine specialist has; for example, the latter must 'keep economic factors in mind and if resources need to be allocated for more urgent things, he should say so.'

Yet again, it is intriguing to find 'allocation of resources' listed together with such sub-headings as suicide attempts, euthanasia, artificial insemination by donor semen and termination of pregnancy (abortion) under the general heading of 'Ethical Dilemmas'. It seems that economics is the science of an ethical dilemma! Particularly interesting is the implication that this dilemma is in some way *extra* ordinary. 'Within the National Health Service, resources are finite, and this may restrict the freedom of the doctor to advise his patient, who will usually be unaware of the limitation'.[23] And the passage continues (with my added emphasis), 'This situation infringes the *ordinary* relationship between patient and doctor.'

There is an acceptance, then, that resources are finite but the proper implications of this are not accepted, perhaps because they are medically unacceptable. Doctors are not charged with *being* efficient and equitable, which is what they ought to be. They are charged with *advising* on efficiency and equity, which they are currently not trained to do. There is some muddled thinking here.

And the muddle gets greater. It is stated that: 'It is clearly the ethical duty of the doctor to use the most economic [sic] and efficacious treatment available.'[24] It is certainly far from clear what an 'economic and efficacious' treatment is and one can only wonder if the members of the BMA understand.

Two of the key features in this are the separation of advice from action and of the individual from the society. The two in fact ought to be linked. Those who are to advise on equity and efficiency ought to do so from a standpoint which is much wider than either the individual patient or indeed the individual practitioner and his patients. There has to be a strong case for those who proffer such advice being separated from the demands and prejudices of individual patient care.

Hence emerges the role of the community physician as stated above but, in a much wider and more important sense, hence the role of the representatives of the society at large no matter who they may be. Issues of equity and efficiency in health care are not the sole ethical province of the medical profession. Indeed, it can be argued that they are not the province of the medical profession outside of community medicine *except* as doers of society's will. In terms of equity and efficiency, clinicians need to be the advised not the advisers.

These are vexed issues. Writing ethical codes is fraught with difficulty. Equity, efficiency and ethics in health care are not solely medical matters; indeed, in many instances in terms of relevant policy making they are not at all medical matters.

Let me exemplify what I mean. If it were the case that the medical profession's values should determine priorities in health care, then would it be wrong to leave the individual members of the profession to make their case to the relevant administrative and political bodies and let resource allocation be based on the strength of the cases put forward? My answer is no but with two provisos: first, that cases be made on a rational basis and, second, that cases be made at the same level of decibels. The men with the muscle are in the acute specialties – the top surgeons and physicians; the weak are in the Cinderella services for the elderly, the mentally ill and handicapped. Left to the individualistic ethics of medicine, the acute sector will tend to win. In terms of justice and allocative efficiency – and therefore in terms of social ethics – it perhaps ought not to. So the fact that power is not fairly distributed within the medical profession makes the members of that august body even less well qualified for advising on justice and efficiency in resource allocation.

These are key issues for the fair and efficient management of health services. They are central to the ethical dilemmas facing health care policy-makers under all sorts of financing and organisational systems. We will return to them again in Chapter 10 after a sojourn into wider issues of equity and ethics; that is, the nature of health care systems and why these vary from country to country.

Notes

1. I am grateful to Elsevier Science Publishers B.V. (Biomedical Division) for permission to reproduce in this chapter parts of my article 'Equity in health care: confronting the confusion', *Effective Health Care*, 1 (1983).
2. L.A. Aday, R. Anderson and G.V. Fleming, *Health Care in the US: Equitable For Whom?* (Sage: Beverly Hills, 1980).
3. N. Daniels, 'Equity of access to health care: some conceptual and ethical issues', *Millbank Memorial Fund Quarterly*, 60 (1982).
4. R. Steele, 'Marginal met need and geographical equity in health care', *Scottish Journal of Political Economy*, 28 (1981).
5. Department of Health and Social Security, *Sharing Resources for Health in England: Report of the Resource Allocation Working Party* (HMSO: London, 1976).
6. R. Carr-Hill, 'RAWP is dead: long live RAWP' in *Competition in Health Care: Reforming the NHS*, eds A.J. Culyer, A.K. Maynard and J.W. Posnett (Macmillan: London, 1990).
7. Department of Health, *Working for Patients*, Cmnd. 555 (HMSO: London, 1989).
8. Department of Health, *Funding and Contracts for Health Services*, Working Paper No. 2 (HMSO: London, 1989a).
9. Carr-Hill, *op. cit.*, p 193.
10. *Ibid.*
11. B. Jarman, 'Identification of underprivileged areas', *British Medical Journal*, 286 (1983), p 705; 'Underprivileged areas: validation and distribution of scores', *British Medical Journal*, 289 (1984), p 1587.
12. J. Hall, 'Equity, access and health', PhD Thesis (University of Sydney: Sydney, 1991).

13. P.A West, 'Theoretical and practical equity in the National Health Service in England', *Social Science and Medicine*, 15 (1981), p 118.
14. G. de Jong and F.F.H. Rutten, 'Justice and health for all', *Social Science and Medicine*, 17 (1983), p 1091.
15. Steele, *op. cit.*
16. I. Kennedy, *The Unmasking of Medicine* (Paladin: London, 1983), p 123.
17. R.M. Veatch, *A Theory of Medical Ethics* (Basic Books: New York, 1980).
18. *Ibid.*, p 258.
19. J. Rawls, *A Theory of Justice* (Oxford University Press: Oxford, 1972).
20. Veatch, *op. cit.*, p 265.
21. British Medical Association, *Handbook of Medical Ethics* (BMA: London, 1984), p 67.
22. *Ibid.*, pp 25–33.
23. *Ibid.*, p 67.
24. *Ibid.*

9

Health care financing and organisation

9.1 Introduction

One of the interesting phenomena in health care in the late twentieth century is how different the financing and organisation arrangements are in different countries. (For a good review see Donaldson and Gerard.[1]) To describe these and highlight their strengths and weaknesses is not the intention of this chapter. Rather, what I want to do here is to examine *why* systems differ. This is a mammoth task. Consequently, in order to constrain it and make the process manageable within the space of one chapter, I have chosen to address the question of why a *national* health service – and to make the question real, why an NHS in the UK?

Fortunately, while this may have a parochial flavour to it, in practice what emerges are messages for all forms of financing and organisation of health care. The messages are principally about equity in the first place, but they are inevitably, given the links that have been established in earlier chapters, also about ethics and efficiency. What health care services attempt to be efficient *about* is a function of the ethical and indeed cultural basis of the society. Change the culture, the ethical base may change, and the goal of efficiency will alter. Indeed it is this, even to a limited extent, that we are witnessing in the NHS reforms. But the key to different health care systems would seem to lie in equity.

In their examination of alternative systems of health care provision, three leading British experts – Culyer, Maynard and

Williams[2] – have suggested that there are essentially two proto-
types of systems. There is system X, which:

> has as its guiding principle consumer sovereignty in a decentralized
> market, in which access to health care is selective according to
> willingness and the ability to pay. It seeks to achieve this sovereignty
> by private insurance; it allows insured services to be available
> partially free at time of consumption; it allows private ownership of
> the means of production and has minimal state control over budgets
> and resource distribution; and it allows the reward of suppliers to be
> determined by the market.

Their other prototype, system Y:

> has as its guiding principle the improvement of health for the
> population at large; it allows selective access according to the
> effectiveness of health care in improving health ('need'). It seeks to
> improve the health of the population at large through a tax-financed
> system free at the point of service. It allows public ownership of the
> means of production subject to central control of budgets; it allows
> some physical direction of resources; and it allows the use of
> countervailing monopsony power to influence the rewards of
> suppliers.

They further suggest, following Donabedian,[3] that it is possible:

> to distinguish sharply between two rival ethical bases, on each of
> which a system of health care can be constructed and justified. The
> first considers access to health care to be essentially similar to access
> to all the other good things in society (food, shelter, leisure
> pursuits); that is, it is part of society's reward system. The second
> regards access to health care as a citizen's right, like access to the
> ballot box or the courts of justice, which should not depend in any
> way on an individual's income and wealth.

The main thrust of the argument of these writers is to examine
each system according to its lights. From their conclusions it is
worth drawing two observations. First, they ask if the two systems
will hybridise and become indistinguishable through convergence
or whether the one has greater power to survive sociopolitical
changes. In response they point to the empirical evidence. Countries which have Y-type systems previously had X-type systems,
whereas they could cite only one example (Australia) which at that
time had gone the other way but has since moved back again. More
recently there is some evidence of a move in the opposite direction

in the UK and the Netherlands. Second, they suggest that the question to be posed is 'whether one is more comfortable with a system in which the discontented minority are the more well-to-do members of society'.[4] They state that 'ultimately, of course, you just have to stand up and be counted'.

I do not want to be critical of this analysis nor its objectives. Indeed, I think that this particular treatment of the 'market versus the state' debate is much more useful than many of its predecessors, particularly in respect of treating different systems in their own lights. Rather, what I want to pose is an additional question which remains unanswered in the analysis by Culyer and his colleagues: why do viewpoints (or 'ethical bases') vary?

To facilitate understanding of this issue, this chapter concentrates attention on the NHS. This is a clear example of a Y-type system based in a country where access to health care is viewed as a citizen's right (i.e. Donabedian's second ethical base). That remains the case if perhaps less so than before the current reforms. The lessons to be drawn are, however, applicable in different ways to all sorts of health care systems, whatever the funding base.

9.2   Key features of the NHS

Different writers, politicians, health care commentators and others have put forward their views on what the objectives of the NHS are, how these differ from other systems and why. For example, Lees has suggested that 'the basic purpose of the NHS is to enforce equality of consumption of medical care'.[5] Culyer, on the other hand, emphasises the relevance of the caring externality, the idea that we care about other people's health, and that it represents a means of allowing individuals to pass to others the responsibility of making decisions about their health care.[6]

Yet, as discussed in more detail later in the chapter, neither of these views appears true for those accepting the revealed-preference school of thought; that is, the idea that individuals or organisations 'reveal' their preferences by the way in which they behave. (An example is the implied-values approach to value of life was discussed in Chapter 5.) There is evidence to suggest that equal health is not what the NHS is about. If it were about equal consumption, it would be very paternalistic, the jibe that some, including Lees, have made against the ethical foundations of the NHS.

Culyer's point regarding passing responsibility to others may have a little more substance to it. It appears to be drawn from Kantian philosophy, where autonomy of the individual to choose, irrespective of any concern by others about whether the choice is right or wrong, good or bad, is paramount.[7] Yet it is far from clear that at the level of the *individual*, as opposed to the community at large, the individual is less or more able to avoid difficult decisions or to abrogate personal responsibility for decision-making under one system than another. Given the agency relationship, such avoidance is not only possible but present under all systems of health care; it appears to be a function of uncertainty regarding illness episodes and treatment availability and effectiveness, and the expected loss if things do go wrong. It is not immediately apparent that any one system is better at reducing uncertainty than any other, except perhaps that under an NHS-type system, for some at least, there is greater certainty of access to health care. The probability of things going wrong may be a function of the system insofar as the effectiveness of care is a function of the system. But the evidence on this is very weak indeed. Clearly, it might be a function of spending on health care, but since this is correlated with income and income in turn with health, this is a blind alley up which it is better not to go.

Rather than conjecture about this, we can look at the evidence of history. On the basis of what the NHS has been doing, has it revealed its preferences? Can we through its behaviour spot what it is that it has been trying to achieve?

Some potentially key concerns of health care systems are:

1. Technological innovation.
2. Equity geographically, by social class.
3. Effectiveness.
4. Efficiency.
5. Professional status.
6. Patients' rights/preferences.
7. Clinicians' rights.
8. Community's preferences.
9. Medical ethics/clinical freedom.

The list is incomplete. On some counts it is impossible at present to make truly informed judgments about strengths and weaknesses across different systems, often because of measurement problems (e.g. effectiveness and consequently efficiency). With others, system and affluence tend to get clogged up together as, for example, in the case of technological innovation. Others, again, seem remarkable in their similarity. As Veatch suggests, medical ethical codes may vary (but it seems not markedly) simply because of different methods of organising and financing health care.[8]

We are left with equity variables, professional status and individual patients' versus the community's rights/preferences – all related to each other since some emphasis on one will tend to mean less weight elsewhere in terms of the values that drive the system. The less sovereign the individual consumer, the higher is professional status. These will be influenced in turn by the community's values, although potentially in different directions. This phenomenon is apparent in the NHS reforms where the attempts to strengthen consumer choice have met with some opposition from the medical profession. The more potent the community feeling the more concern, *ceteris paribus*, will there be with equity. Given the central importance of the potency of the community feeling, equity and the relationship between these, the rest of this chapter will be devoted to these issues.

Equity, as highlighted in Chapter 8, can be and has been defined in many ways in health care. All of the definitions identified have equality in common; most are dependent on defining need in some way or other; all have been the subject of some confusion.

It is difficult to determine which, if any, of them is in any sense the 'right' definition. Clearly, such a judgment is value-laden unless, of course, it is already laid down in law or custom that some lexicographic priority is to be given to equity over all other possible goals or objectives.

An important value judgment here relates to the relative weight to be attached to equity *vis-à-vis* efficiency. For example, equality of access for equal need, if pursued in full, will almost inevitably result in inefficiency in the sense of less health being provided than could be from the resources available; for example, providing sophisticated in-patient care in all areas of a country will promote more equal access but potentially less health for a given budget.

These issues were dealt with in detail in the last chapter. Here I want to consider more fundamentally the question, raised earlier in this chapter, of why the viewpoints on which health care systems are based differ, with the focus here specifically on the community's preferences and the weight attached to equity.

9.3   Fair shares for all?

Normally, the expression 'fair shares for all' is thought of in terms of the distribution of some set of goods or services which is declared just in terms of society at large or some sub-group. It is thus about giving out good things fairly.

In an interesting (but for some readers a potentially difficult) way of thinking about social policy, Margolis has turned this standard way of viewing fair shares for all around.[9] He considers fair-sharing as not what one gets but what one does; that is, he sees it as *doing* one's fair share rather than *getting* one's fair share. He seizes on the fact that we are all to a greater or lesser extent social and political animals and that we view ourselves not just as individuals with the ability to enjoy the good things of this life. Additionally, we want to do our 'fair share' for the society, the community, the group, the family – at least some set of individuals wider than but including our individual selves.

The motivation for this willingness to 'do our bit' is not based on the output from our actions in helping or assisting the group; it is the action per se that generates the utility which serves as the motivation. It is the knowledge that we are participating that counts.

Altruism? Perhaps, but not in a pure form since Margolis stresses that in participating in the group and devoting resources to the group we as individuals are equal members of the group. Also, the motivation is not strictly or directly to help others. It is not so much feeling useful as feeling good through group participation.

His 'fair shares model' (FS model) is developed in the context of social policy generally. Here I want to describe his approach in some detail and then show how it applies to health care – indeed, how it applies better to health care than other rationales for equity that have been proposed. (For an additional brief outline of this see Culyer;[10] for a more detailed explanation see Hall.[11]) Thereafter

I want to draw some conclusions based on the explanatory power of Margolis' model.

The basic postulate on which Margolis builds his approach is that individuals obtain utility (satisfaction) in two ways: one in the normal (economic) sense of getting satisfaction from the goods and services that we consume — the form of utility we encountered in Chapter 2 in the explanation of demand. The other way — and this is the novel aspect — is through *participation* in group-orientated activities. The utility derived from this group-related activity is not directly a function of either the utility of the output the individual receives as an equal member of the group or the utility of the output which the group receives. However, the willingness of individuals to participate is in part a function of the degree of efficiency with which the group-orientated activities are organised as perceived by the individual. In other words, individuals are more willing to take part in efficient groups or efficient group activities than inefficient ones. Thus, the utility in this second form is process rather than output utility: it is the doing rather than what is given or received that counts.

The individual splits his resources between activities through which he obtains utility selfishly and those through which he obtains utility as a result of participating in the group. As is usual in utility theory, the individual attempts to maximise his utility, which means ensuring that the sum of the S-utility (selfish utility) and group-participation utility is the greatest possible. Thus, if the individual can get even greater utility from using some of his resources to participate more in group-orientated activities than spending them on himself, then he will do so. Such switches of resources will continue until the individual cannot increase his total utility any more. At this point he will have the optimum balance between his allocations to the self and to the group.

Unless pure altruism does lie behind fair-sharing, then the least selfish individuals in society run the risk of being exploited by the more selfish. The likelihood of this is of course dependent on the different degrees of selfishness individuals have within the group (or society). If all are equally selfish (and hence equally selfless), then there will be no exploitation and a stable situation will obtain. However, this is most unlikely. How then can the potential for exploitation be removed or reduced?

Margolis suggests that his 'participation ratio', which is a function of the ratio of spending to obtain group participation utility and spending to obtain S-utility, would not be constant for each individual. Rather it would vary in that the more an individual had already allocated to the group, the less he would want to participate still more in the group.

Although that is in essence what the FS model is about, for those interested it is worth expanding the explanation a little more technically, through the use of two diagrams. On the vertical axis in Figure 9.1 are measured the marginal utility of the individual's allocation to himself, S', and the marginal utility, *as perceived by the individual*, of the group's spending, G' (note, not of the individual's allocation to the group). On the horizontal axis is the individual's resource allocation to selfish activities (i.e. s which has a maximum value of I, the individual's income).

It should be noted in Figure 9.1 that as the individual devotes more and more of his resources to selfish ends (i.e. as s moves outwards towards I), there is *no* impact on G'. However, G' is influenced by the individual's perception of the marginal utility to the group (of which he is an equal member) of the aggregate resources for group interest. Thus, G_1' is higher than G_2' because, independently of his contribution to the group, the individual perceives the marginal productivity of the *group's* resources to be higher in the former case than the latter. (If you have a choice of contributing

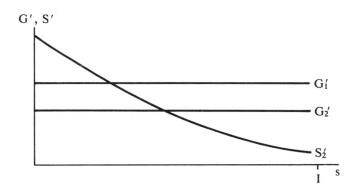

Figure 9.1 Marginal utility (G') of the group's resources allocated to group interest and marginal utility (S') of Smith's resources allocated to selfish interest (s), $s + g = I$, g equals Smith's allocation to the group and I equals Smith's income

to one of two organisations, one of which you perceive as being efficient and the other inefficient, *ceteris paribus*, which will you chose?)

In the second diagram, Figure 9.2, the key to the model is contained in the two functions presented there. First, G'/S', the 'value ratio', is the ratio of marginal G-utility *as perceived by the individual* and marginal S-utility to the individual. Now, from Figure 9.1 we know that G' is unaffected by the individual's allocation between group and self-interest. But S' is so affected; as the individual devotes more and more of his income to self-interest, so the marginal utility of his self-interested activities will fall. (This is based on the simple principle introduced in Chapter 2 of 'diminishing marginal utility', i.e. the more you have the less you value an extra unit.) Consequently, as the individual devotes more and more of his income to selfish ends (i.e. as s moves closer to I), so S' will fall and, since G' is constant throughout, G'/S' will rise, as in Figure 9.2. The 'participation ratio', W, is wholly a function of the act of participating. Utility here is in the act not the outcome. But the more the individual acts in the group interest – that is, the

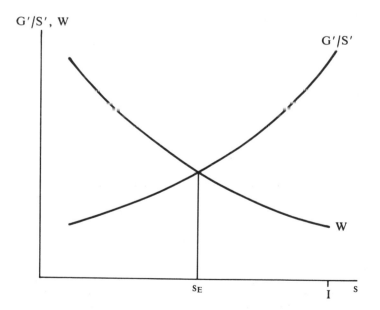

Figure 9.2 Equilibrium of G'/S' and W

more of his income he devotes to the group – the less is the marginal utility of devoting still more. Consequently, as the individual devotes more and more to selfish ends (and less and less to group ends), so the participation ratio, which is a function of the ratio of the individual's spending on group participation utility and spending on S-utility, will fall (see Figure 9.2).

The individual is thus maximising his combined utility, both in the S-utility form and the participation form, at s_E, that is, he allocates s_E to selfish activities and $I - s_E$ to group activities.

9.4 Fair-sharing and health care

What is the relevance of this model to health care systems? Essentially, it would seem that, following Culyer, Maynard and Williams,[12] health care systems sit on a spectrum which stretches in principle at least from the individualistic, market orientated, part-of-the-reward-system type of organisation on the one hand to, on the other, a paternalistic, equitable, needs-based organisation. What Margolis' model does is to allow us to see these different systems in the dimensions of group-participation utility and S-utility. Thus, to the extent that a society is composed of individuals who find their equilibrium between selfish utility and group participation to be very much at the selfish utility/low participation end, then it will be the market-orientated system of health care that will dominate. If individuals are of the type who are keen to participate and play down selfish utility, then the NHS-type system will more likely obtain.

Readers may find it a little difficult to accept this rationale for the emergence of different systems in different counties. To help them I have raised three specific explanations of the NHS below and tried to show how Margolis' approach can provide a better rationale than the others.

9.5 Other explanations of the NHS

(i) *Lees*

In the early 1960s Lees argued that 'the basic purpose of the NHS is to enforce equality of consumption of medical care'.[13] He suggested that this was 'the one logically necessary, intellectually defensible purpose of the NHS' in which 'a single ... set of preferences is formulated at the centre and then applied uniformly to all who use the NHS'.

Lees thus stated quite explicitly that equity was the goal of the NHS – and I would not necessarily dispute that – but that it was equity as defined by equality of consumption of health care. Despite the considerable confusion that exists in this area, I am not aware of any government or NHS policy documents which embrace the concept of 'equal consumption' although some interpretations would suggest that this was at least implied by the famous (or infamous) Black Report. [14] (This report on inequalities in health across different socioeconomic groups highlighted the continuing gap in health status between rich and poor. It indicated even more the gap in concern about the issue between the two main political parties. The report was commissioned by a Labour government and completed under a Conservative government. Only after major criticism from many different groups – including the medical press – was the original print-run of less than 300 copies expanded.) It would seem more accurate in any case to view the Black Report as concerned with *health* inequalities rather than health care consumption inequalities, especially as the report recognised explicitly that there was a limit to what the health service could do to narrow health differentials across the social classes.

While it is difficult to accept Lees' explanation, none the less his comments on primary and secondary poverty are more acceptable. In the setting up of the NHS, he saw the abandonment of prices as the decisive step (a comment with which certainly I would disagree), and for two key reasons. First, he challenges the primary poverty argument on the basis that medical care could be taken care of in the same way as we try to ensure that the poor get enough of other 'essentials' – food, clothing, housing, and so on (i.e. largely through cash payments to supplement income). Second, he challenges the secondary poverty argument on the grounds that this cannot be solved by making health insurance compulsory. On these points his arguments are sound; whether subsidies, cash payments and compulsory health insurance are *better* mechanisms is another matter. Certainly, however, the removal of prices is not unique to a national health service, and a national health service is, *inter alia*, a compulsory health insurance system.

(ii)   *Culyer*

First and foremost, Culyer suggests that it is on the supply side that
the main justification for an NHS exists;[15] that is, simply on
grounds of *efficiency*, given the objectives of provision of approved
treatments and giving priority to those in greatest need, a publicly
owned system is likely to be preferred over some complex system
of subsidies. Interestingly, and I will return to the issue in Chapter
10, he also comments that the NHS has never been 'provided with
the set of approved technologies and proper priorities ... that constitute its principal (indeed its sole) justification'. Certainly, this *is*
an important issue, but if it were the sole or principal justification,
given that it has not occurred, then it would be difficult to understand how the NHS has survived for over forty years.

Culyer has in fact three other supporting arguments for the
NHS. In circumstances where a community's values are relatively
homogeneous it represents a reasonable means of ensuring that a
single set of preferences applies. I would endorse this view.
However, it is more difficult to accept his view that part of the
justification for the NHS is that it also represents a means of allowing individuals to pass to others the responsibility about their
health care. This would seem to be true for *all* health care systems,
at least at the level of the individual *qua* individual. However – and
it does not seem to be Culyer's point – if we reinterpret this to
mean that the NHS represents a means of allowing the *community*
to pass to others the responsibility about the *community's* health
care, then this does seem to be potentially an important role for the
NHS. The extent to which it performs it in practice would seem to
be deficient.

Finally, there is the caring externality. As Culyer describes it,
'One individual is not affected merely by the possibility of another
passing some disease on to him ... but also, and much more importantly, by the state of health of the other in itself. Individuals are
affected by others' health status for the simple reason that most of
them care.'[16] This concept of a caring externality is prevalent in the
literature on social policy generally. However, beyond the Black
Report, there is no evidence to suggest that in terms of policy the
NHS is about equalising health. The caring externality may exist,
but the revealed preference of the NHS does not point to its being
in the dimension of health or health status.

(iii) *Titmuss*

In 1970 Titmuss published his book *The Gift Relationship*, which showed that supplying blood through a process of voluntary donation (as in the UK) was more effective and almost certainly more efficient than the commercial process used in the United States.[17] However, while the empirical evidence seemed to support him on this front, it was the wider aspects of his book (subtitled *From Human Blood to Social Policy*) which provoked greater controversy. He wrote:[18] 'Altruism in giving to a stranger does not begin and end with blood donations. It may touch every aspect of life ... it is likely that a decline in the spirit of altruism in one sphere of human activities will be accompanied by similar changes in attitudes, motives and relationships elsewhere.'

It was from this sentiment that he went on to describe the establishment of the NHS in the following terms: 'The most unsordid act of British social policy in the twentieth century has allowed and encouraged sentiments of altruism, reciprocity and social duty to express themselves; to be made explicit and identifiable in measurable patterns of behaviour by all social groups and classes.'

Many commentators have disagreed or at least been sceptical about this wider theme of Titmuss; see, for example, Arrow.[19] However, for a partial defence, see Collard.[20] Essentially, the debate here centres around whether the stock of altruism is scarce (Arrow's view) or, as Singer suggests,[21] more like sexual potency: the more you use it, the better it is. For our purposes, however, it is more important to note that Collard's neat defence of Titmuss is, in essence, Kantian. He suggests that the 'non-Kantian altruist' will recognise that his donation is so small as to affect negligibly the probability of someone in need of getting a blood transfusion. And if everyone adopts this attitude, voluntary blood donation will be small or non-existent. Collard states that to defend Titmuss:[22]

> one is driven back ... to the notion that potential donors ... behave Kantianly. They reason that, although the effect of their own individual failure to donate would be negligible, the effect of 'everyone' behaving like this would cause [the probability that some randomly drawn individual would be able to get a blood transfusion] to fall towards zero. They have a duty or responsibility to give blood.

Now, one potential problem here is that economists are generally suspicious of Kant and his emphasis on responsibility and duty, on grounds that if these take on a categorical imperative form, choice, which is centre stage for the economist, is redundant. Collard stresses, however, that this Kantian behaviour is only one element in the utility function, and it is 'tradeable' in the sense that 'the marginal donor could well be discouraged by an increase in the "time and trouble" costs of giving'.

Despite his protestation, it is clear that Titmuss saw the NHS as a morally superior form of organisation of health care, not primarily because of what it delivers by way of health but what it does to promote altruism. Whatever one's views are on whether or not to support Titmuss in these conjectures, in terms of justifying the NHS it would be unfortunate if we had to rely solely on the argument that whatever its merits in terms of health, it was better at delivering altruism. There is also much to be said for being rid of Kant. Despite Collard's caveats, there is a sense in which duty and responsibility are a means of opting out of choices. That may be an unjust view, but there is a clear advantage in avoiding the issue completely.

Where does this leave Margolis? Essentially, it leaves him out of step with Lees, with almost certainly mixed feelings towards Culyer and with considerable sympathy towards Titmuss. The fact that Margolis is out of step with Lees is not a problem, since there is little if any empirical evidence to support Lees' prime contention that the NHS is about equal consumption. Culyer overplays the supply-side issue but it has its echoes in Margolis in his view that because of the high search costs involved in achieving efficiency and a single set of preferences, coercion (nationalisation) may be an efficient solution for looking after the group's interest and thereby promoting G', the marginal utility of the group. Indeed, it is likely that Margolis would endorse the idea that the NHS represents a means whereby the *community* (and not individuals as Culyer would have it) can pass to a single body the responsibility for the community's health. On the caring externality there is a parallel with the idea of group utility. However, the issue of participation seems to win in practice in that the evidence supports the view that the NHS's equity goal is couched in terms of access rather than health or, indeed, health care consumption. Access for the group is essentially what Margolis is about: beyond that utilisation and health involve S-utility resources, a point which appears to be at least implicitly accepted in NHS policy.

Finally, Margolis is at pains to point out that he is not concerned with any ethical aspect with which some might imbue his fair-shares model but simply how well it explains how people behave. Margolis is thus set firmly in utilitarianism, so avoiding all the problems encountered by Titmuss with Kant, duty and responsibility and the moral posturing which Titmuss tends to bring to his analysis. The issue is then one of which theory best reflects the equity goals of the NHS. Since these are couched in terms of equality of access, both Lees and Culyer are less valid empirically than Margolis. There is little difference that is measurable empirically between Margolis and Titmuss.

Get rid of Kant and duty and there is little difference between the two in principle. Maybe for some that doesn't matter; for others, like myself, to believe that people behave as they do, not out of duty, but because they want to behave that way (i.e. they are utilitarians) has considerable appeal. (Or maybe it's not so much a question of dropping duty but rather dropping the notion of a moral imperative and just accepting that there is utility in doing our duty.)

I would therefore conclude on the basis of this discussion that the factor which primarily separates out different health care systems is equity, defined probably in terms of some concept of equality of access. Where participation altruism *à la* Margolis is strong and there is a relatively homogeneous set of preferences in a society then the health care financing system is likely to be at the NHS-end of the spectrum. Where concern for individual utility is of prime interest to the citizens of a country and freedom of choice fosters heterogeneity of preferences, more market-orientated health care systems will tend to prevail. It is not a complete explanation by any means but looking at the UK and Denmark on the one hand and the United States on the other would seem to provide some empirical support for this explanation of why health care financing systems differ.

9.6 Other insights from Margolis

Finally this chapter discusses briefly two other aspects of Margolis' model which seem to provide useful insights into the nature of health care systems.

(i)   *Isn't the caring externality enough? Is fair-sharing different?*

If individuals care about others in the sense of caring about their access to health care, can't we replace fair-sharing with this caring externality? Certainly, caring about access and fair-sharing are very similar but caring about access might not get us beyond compulsory health insurance for all. Also, the notion of 'fair-sharing' can be explained more satisfactorily (wanting to do my bit for my fellow man, provided he does his bit for me) than can the caring externality. In the context of our attitudes to self-induced disease (e.g. smoking-induced bronchitis), fair-sharing seems a more appropriate base for the analysis than the caring externality. The latter appears incapable of distinguishing one bronchitic from another; the former can because of the concern permitted about exploitation of the group interest − essentially here the fact that as a result of one individual's overindulgence in S-interest (i.e. smoking) the costs may fall on the group and the community's G-interest may thereby be diminished.

Strictly, too, fair-sharing does not involve an externality at all. This is because the utility derived by individuals outside of S-utility is through participation. Thus, total utility is the sum of all individuals' S-utilities plus the sum of all individuals' utilities derived from participating in the group. To include the utility derived by the group from the resources allocated to the group (which is what the externality would normally be considered to be) would involve an element of double counting.

(ii)   *Why in health care?*

Potentially this gets us back into the debate (see Chapter 3) about whether, in what ways and to what extent health care is different from other commodities. The 'whether' question seems to be answered yes, given the extent of the empirical evidence showing that health care markets do seem to be rather different from others.

Regarding the question 'what ways?', the key elements I would suggest are two and related: first, consumers' lack of knowledge of the commodity and, second, the near monopoly position of the medical profession regarding this very same knowledge. One way of acknowledging the potential for problems in this asymmetric world of knowledge is to have the state as the final arbiter with respect to the profession controlling information in health care (i.e. the medical profession). As individuals we are ignorant with regard to health care, therefore we are weak. This can be dealt with in one of two ways. First, attempt to strengthen the power of the consumer through increased competition, for example as is being attempted in the NHS reforms. Clearly something can be done to give consumers better information – but not sufficient in my view, or at least not sufficient to allow us to have it at a cost which would make the process worthwhile. Consequently, the second approach seems preferable. Our best defence is in the power of the state; hence nationalisation. The question of 'to what extent?' is a cultural value judgment. The greater is this concern to control the medical profession – the more often the question 'quis custodiet ipsos custodes?' is posed – the less market regulation is accepted as a feasible solution, and the greater the homogeneity of values in a society, the more likely the health service will be nationalised.

These arguments could be extended. Yet there seems enough here to believe that the Margolis model can go a long way to help to explain not only the structure of different health care systems but also why they differ in different societies.

Notes

1. C. Donaldson and K. Gerard, *The Visible Hand: The Economics of Health Care Financing* (Macmillan: London, 1992).
2. A.J. Culyer, A. Maynard and A. Williams, 'Alternative systems of health care provision: an essay on motes and beams' in *A New Approach to the Economics of Health Care*, ed. M. Olson (American Enterprise Institute: Washington and London, 1981), p 134.
3. A. Donabedian, 'Social responsibility for personal health services: an examination of basic values', *Inquiry*, 8 (1971).
4. Culyer, *et al.*, *op. cit.*, p 149.
5. D.S. Lees, 'The logic of the British National Health Service', *Journal of Law and Economics*, 5 (1962), p 116.

6. A.J. Culyer, *Need and the National Health Service* (Martin Robertson: London, 1976).

7. I. Kant, *The Critique of Pure Reason* (Macmillan: New York and London, 1934).

8. R.M. Veatch, *A Theory of Medical Ethics* (Basic Books: New York, 1980).

9. H. Margolis, *Selfishness, Altruism and Rationality* (Cambridge University Press: London, 1982).

10. A.J. Culyer, 'The normative economics of health care finance and provision' in *Providing Health Care: The Economics of Alternative Systems of Finance and Delivery,* eds A. McGuire, P. Fenn and K. Mayhew (Oxford University Press: Oxford, 1991).

11. J. Hall, 'Equity in health care', PhD Thesis (University of Sydney: Sydney, 1991).

12. Culyer *et al.*, *op. cit.*

13. Lees, *op. cit.*, p 116.

14. Report of a Research Working Group, *Inequalities in Health* (Department of Health and Social Security, London, 1980) – The 'Black Report'.

15. Culyer, 1976, *op. cit.*, p 93.

16. *Ibid.*, p 89.

17. R.M. Titmuss, *The Gift Relationship* (Allen and Unwin: London, 1970).

18. *Ibid.*, p 198.

19. K.J. Arrow, 'Gifts and exchanges', *Philosophy and Public Affairs,* 1 (1974).

20. D. Collard, *Altruism and Economy* (Martin Robertson: Oxford, 1978).

21. P. Singer, 'Altruism and commerce: a defence of Titmuss against Arrow', *Philosophy and Public Affairs,* 2 (1973).

22. Collard, *op. cit.*, p 142.

10

Future challenges

Quis custodiet ipsos custodes?

10.1 Introduction

Where does this leave us? Basically in something of a turmoil is the most accurate answer. In many ways economics *is* the dismal science in that its analysis of existing health care is far from joyous.[1] But the silver lining is that if the will is there, the situation can be improved through the use of economics.

Beyond the ideas put forward in the previous chapter, I have endeavoured to avoid the polemics of the collectivist versus the market debate. For the majority of practitioners, that in any case is not the issue. However, it may be important to emphasise that most commentators agree that there is no solution at the level of the grand design. All systems have their inefficiencies in practice; all systems are capable of being made more efficient and almost certainly, where desired, more equitable.

This point is worth dwelling on for a moment. As reported by McLachlan and Maynard, 'that perceptive economist Uve Reinhardt has observed that there are currently three desiderata which universally dominate health goals: equity, provider freedom to price and practice; and budgetary and economic control'.[2] As these commentators add, 'the vast majority of the population would elect for equity to be the prime consideration'. I would agree.

By now it should be clear to the reader that if he is interested in the pursuit of a healthy population and a fair distribution of health (or access to health care) within that population, then economic analysis, in principle at least, is on the side of the angels. In practice, and in its frequent misuse, it is certainly not surprising that economics gets a bad press in health care. That is largely the fault of economists. Beyond that, the faults for what is currently happening lie elsewhere.

Too often, as societies, we have got health care policy wrong. Much depends on the expectations of the public; this varies from country to country. Yet little is done in any country to adjust the public's expectations to more reasonable levels. Much also depends on the medical profession; they seem to vary little from country to country. We need to do more to restrain in particular the acute clinicians, especially in their romantic endeavours. The caricature of the clinician, armed with the sword of clinical freedom, and clothed in the armour of self-righteousness, protected (from serious thought processes) by the mythical shield of infinite resources, attempting to save the world from death and disease, we can do without. We can and should all respect their skills in the operating theatre and the intensive care unit. It is less apparent that we should laud them if they attempt to lead the monotechnic charge on the way to health for all. Of course, doctors have a right to promote health care and to give hope to their patients. As they do so, however, it is worth noting that they may not do so solely for reasons of altruism.

Equity in health care means much more to society at large than to doctors. Certainly, it comes at a cost. But in the context of health care, is the opportunity cost of greater equity really too high? Has the last 0.5 per cent of GNP devoted to supposedly better health care been justified rather than being devoted to more equal access? I don't know the answers to these questions. My point is that we need more often to get round to posing them.

In this concluding chapter I want to spell out some of the ways that, as an economist, I consider might be pursued to try to ensure more efficient, equitable health care. There is no single solution, but getting widespread agreement to an objective of fair and efficient delivery of health for the community would get us quite a long way down the road towards a solution. I will then consider the extent to which the NHS reforms can or might lead to more efficient, equitable health care (although given the time of writing – June 1991 – such judgments are difficult).

10.2 Education

It is wrong to blame the people in the health care system for their lack of use of economics and understanding of this discipline if they have never been taught even the basics. Daily the health service journals, health policy statements and health care plans abound with misperceptions about and lack of awareness of things economic. Worse, there is a downright distrust and suspicion of this noble discipline, especially among clinicians.

Clearly, these attitudes have to be changed, and where better to start than with undergraduate medical education. In all health care systems doctors have to be managers, especially hospital clinicians, even if many doctors do not appreciate the fact. Yet the extent to which they are trained in management skills, such as economics, is minimal.

In evaluating the teaching of economics to medical undergraduates in the University of Aberdeen, a frequent response from the students is 'it's not us you want to get at, it's the consultants'. Agreed; but how do we get at the consultants?

It is not a rhetorical question. There is a need to educate consultants in some basic economics. Perhaps first, however, there is a need to *sell* them economics. Once some of the medical profession get themselves to the top of the ladder, when there is no longer any risk in climbing, they can and do act as excellent salesmen for economics – especially to their fellows in the medical trade.

There is little reason why just a little economics could not be taught in all medical schools as a compulsory, examinable subject. (According to the Aberdeen students, there are other seminars they would be prepared to forgo in order to have more economics.) Certainly, no senior registrar should be allowed to take up a consultant post without *some* knowledge from say a one-week course in economics. For someone about to run a business with a turnover in the UK of well over £0.5 million a year, a minimum of one week's compulsory training in economics would not go amiss.

But education should not stop at the medical profession. Most senior nurses in my experience are already skilled in amateur economics. At least they are aware of the principles and the practice of trying to do the best they can with the resources available. They need more formal training, especially before entering management; but in terms of their awareness, and amenability to learn economics, they are some way ahead of most of their medical colleagues.

Administrators and finance staff often have some knowledge of economics. It is usually less than is adequate for the tasks they face. Health service management – and it seems to be an international problem – is low in status, requisite skills and appropriate training. A training in economics can't solve all these deficiencies, but there are worse places to start.

Perhaps most important of all, there are the customers – the public at large, the patients and the politicians. For all these groups there is a general need for health service education in order to allow reality to win in health care debates. Such health service education needs some basis in economics.

Finally, there is a need to educate economists. In all countries there is currently a shortage of trained health economists. We need more of them. The best way to get our fellow economists interested is to offer them the right incentives.

This shortage of health economists is becoming more and more of a problem. While increasingly health planners and managers seek economists' advice and more health service personnel apply for courses in health economics, the supply of health economists expands all too slowly. There is a need for more undergraduate exposure to health economics in economics faculties and more widespread opportunities to train in health economics at a post-graduate level.

10.3   Information

Writing specifically about the NHS, Maynard suggests that 'there is no information about specialty costs, there is little evaluation of the process of providing care or the outputs, if any, of the caring process, and the idea of quality evaluation is regarded as novel and radical'.[3] Certainly, where there is a billing system either to the patient or a third-party payer, information on costing tends to be better; on evaluation and outputs it is much the same as in the NHS.

As Maynard goes on, 'The production of such information will enable all health care actors, doctors, nurses, physiotherapists and others, to establish explicit professional standards of practice. The establishment of standards or norms of practice would enable the profession to use peer review and medical audit systems to ensure that professionals adhered in their everyday practice to the standards of their trade.'

Information, cost consciousness, monitoring of performance and standards, evaluation of care, planning – all are poor but the NHS reforms (see below) give hope of improvements on some of these fronts. There is little point in economists indulging in beating doctors over the head because of their inefficiencies if the doctors do not have the information available on which they themselves can judge their efficiency.

What evidence exists suggests that providing cost information alone, unless it directly affects the doctor, will have little effect on doctor efficiency. Wickings *et al.* found from their own study that 'disseminating costing data alone produces few changes'.[4] They also suggested that 'there is a disappointing lack of evidence that other clinical costing studies, if they have not been accompanied by powerful educational programmes or by budgeting systems, have achieved improvements in efficiency'.

This is understandable. To expect otherwise can only be as a result of a false understanding of what constitutes appropriate cost information. It is not particularly informative to tell a young child that he can't have a lollipop because it costs 50p. Tell him that he can have two ice-creams for the price of this lollipop and he'll get the message very quickly. So cost information per se is not the answer; it is awareness of *opportunity cost* that matters. *That* has to be the message of exercises to provide cost information. Related to this is the fact that cost information in a 'no choice' situation is at best irrelevant, at worst confusing. Even in a choice situation, as indicated in Chapter 2, it is necessary to ensure that we've got the right cost information.

To place all the emphasis on cost information would, however, play into the hands of those who think that economics is only about costs and about cutting costs. Just as important, for those who understand the concept of opportunity cost, is the output or benefit side. It is here – as was discussed in Chapter 4 – that the real challenge of measurement lies. Fortunately, from the point of view of improving the state of the applied art of health status measurement, what currently occurs is so poor, in some situations nonexistent, that there is scope for great optimism here.

It would help even more if the scientific journals and, before them, the research funders took a much more rigorous line in vetting research and its findings. It is not good enough to know that method A diagnoses better than method B. We want to know *how* much better and what the implications are for treatment and thereby health status as a result of better diagnosis. Nor is it enough to know that cancer patients treated with chemotherapy have a 50 per cent chance of survival for five years. What we want to know is what effect, impact for *change*, the treatment has – and not just on life expectation. So much could be done here; so little is. Even the little that is seems too often to be ignored. For example, in the case of heart attacks, as Hampton[5] has remarked, and as quoted previously in Chapter 5, 'Although the value of prophylactic treatment of infarct survivors with a beta blocker has been better investigated than almost any treatment for any cardiovascular problem, this treatment has not yet become part of routine clinical practice.'

Output at the clinical level can be better measured as can effectiveness. And not just at the clinical level. For example, a wealth of knowledge exists regarding what happens if women have a breast removed. Let's pull all that knowledge together and make it generally available for the betterment of womankind – and the betterment of knowledge of doctors who currently pontificate on whether or not to remove a breast. Outputs can often be measured in terms of mortality and morbidity; when it proves impossible to do so, let's use informed corporate guesses (often called 'consensus conferences'). I would rather be operated on on the basis of an informed guess corporately made by the medical profession as a whole or general surgeons as a whole or neurosurgeons as a whole than on the guess, even informed, of one individual surgeon.

One particularly important issue with regard to clinical decision-making that has become of increased significance in recent years is that of medical practice variations. Even in a small country like Denmark with a population of 5 million there are enormous variations geographically in the rates at which various common procedures are conducted. For example, there are 6-fold variations in hysterectomy rates across the different hospital catchment areas (Andersen *et al.*, 1987[6]). But similar pictures emerge for all countries and most procedures investigated.

These variations are the result of various influences, but what is now very clear is that a large part is due to differences in the way that doctors practise. Doctors simply are not agreed as to what is best medical practice. While in economic terms it is clear that best medical practice ought to be equated with efficient practice (with some allowance for equity), it is not at all clear from the literature what the medical criteria are for defining best medical practice. Given the lack of knowledge (even if not their fault) of doctors of the costs of their activities and the apparent lack of knowledge of the effectiveness of their treatments, or at least disagreement about effectiveness, it is hardly surprising that such variations in medical practice exist. It is surprising that the variations are allowed to continue. It is a situation that we would not accept from our plumbers and one that most doctors would not accept from their secretaries.

Yet knowledge of these variations is not new. It has existed for over 50 years. The problem, however, as Evans[7] has described it, is simple. 'Knowing is not the same as doing.' There is here a serious problem for all health care services and it is a problem which, although it originates with medical science, is then, in terms of its continuance, the responsibility of policy-makers and politicians. It is they who must try to ensure the effective and efficient use of society's scarce resources in health care. But then it is not always too clear precisely who such people are.

There is also the issue of management information. The extent to which managers in one country know what is going on in another is very limited. Yet as the problems are often quite remarkably similar, so might be the solutions. Giving out cost information to clinicians has been tried in a number of countries. Can we not learn internationally from that? Measuring effectiveness of clinical treatments is an international industry, information about which is unconstrained by national boundaries. Measuring effectiveness of management 'treatments' is similarly an international industry, yet many managers, at least in the NHS, appear not to know what is going on even in the adjoining district and show little interest in looking to other countries. However, there are signs of change in this respect. Apart from other changes, the NHS reforms appear to have engendered a greater interest in how other countries are managing their health care systems.

Finally, a word is appropriate about too much information or using information as a substitute for thought. An enormous amount of routine data is collected in all health care systems. Yet when I go to look for information relevant to some specific problem I am analysing, more often than not I find I have to generate my own data. Am I alone? I don't think so, and consequently a note of caution is relevant. There is a need to monitor routinely collected data to see if anyone is actually using it for some good purpose. If not, then need it be collected routinely at all? All data collection has a cost; that needs to be weighed up against the expected value of its use. Too infrequently does this happen. Information too ought to be seen as an aid to planning, evaluation and management and not as a substitute for them. There has to be a good case for thinking about what is to be done with data *before* collecting them. This might lead to the collection of different data, less or none. I would therefore not want my plea for more information to be taken as a blank cheque for health care information systems officers to extend their empires without thought for either the cost or the benefit of their activities. A particularly good (or bad?) example of this phenomenon is the issue of needs assessment, which has become public health's main pillar in the NHS reforms. It is an issue that will be discussed in greater detail below.

10.4 Evaluation and monitoring

Evaluation and monitoring may be simply other forms of information, but the issues surrounding them seem sufficiently important to warrant a separate section on their own. One problem here is that the words themselves mean all things to all men. Evaluation to me means four things:

1. Is this worth doing in terms of doing any good? Is it effective?
2. Is it worth doing it this way rather than that? What is more cost-effective?
3. Is it worth doing given the opportunity cost involved? Are the benefits greater than the costs?
4. Is it worth doing more? Are the benefits of more greater than the costs of more?

Monitoring means checking afterwards to see whether what was thought before turned out to be right – and if not, why not. Consequently, monitoring can lead to not just seeing whether we got it right but also increasing the probability of getting it more right in the future through improving our evaluation methods. Unfortunately, many clinical evaluations seem to address the wrong question or at least questions that are too narrowly focused. Perhaps this is understandable. More money needs to be made available for studies in evaluation and monitoring, but unless the money and the research are heavily policed, then 'more' (if it comes from a vested interest like the drug industry) will not automatically mean 'better'. (By all means, place the cost of evaluation on the industry, but let's ensure that the evaluations are conducted on the four issues raised above. There may be squeals from the pharmaceutical industry, but even they – at least one company: Smith, Kline – have attempted to mount a series of economic appraisal studies.)

One of the biggest advantages of using economic appraisal techniques, beyond the appraisal itself and the promotion of efficiency, is that it encourages decision-makers to think – to think more explicitly about the problem (defining that currently is a major step), to think more comprehensively about possible solutions, to think more coherently about both the advantageous and disadvantageous effects and to think more lucidly about what weights to attach to these effects, who should appropriately do this and how. In turn, a second advantage follows from this; namely, if all this process has been gone through prior to the decision being made, it is far more likely that the decision will be right and can more readily be seen to be right and, consequently and importantly, much more readily implemented. There are powerful forces at work within the health care system, not all of which necessarily subscribe both to the objective of maximising the health of the population in a fair way and to the acceptance of resource constraints. Coherent, systematic decision-making makes it more difficult to get decisions wrong; it also makes it more difficult to attack good decisions on a wrong basis.

On values, as part of evaluation, we need to re-examine medical ethics and in particular the way in which clinical freedom operates in both principle and practice. It is a laudable objective: doing the best one can for one's patients. It is, after all, what the individual consumer's sovereignty often demands. More recognition needs to be taken, however, of the aggregate citizenry's sovereignty. There is a balance here which has to be struck — and struck better than is currently the case.

There can be little doubt that many doctors would suggest that it is their right and duty to defend clinical freedom, believing that if they don't, if they swallow the edicts of economics, then the resources that society will be prepared to devote to health care will fall. Insofar as they see themselves able to defend spending on health care, then they will attempt to do so. This is very human yet potentially romantic or monotechnic. It is romantic if it is done on the basis of not accepting that there may be an opportunity cost which is greater than the health benefits obtained. It is monotechnic if it accepts the opportunity cost but argues that health is what matters and all other demands on resources are secondary. Beer and cigarettes versus health provides the lexicographic slogan which denies rational thinking — especially at the margin where it matters.

The issue here is too important to be left to the doctors. As a society, we have given them the training to allow us efficiently to have medical knowledge available to us. But the medical profession must serve the society that created them. If we educate them better, perhaps they will better understand the social milieu in which they operate. The final responsibility rests with us as citizens not with the profession.

Certainly, one place to start is with the way in which clinical freedom operates and is interpreted. One doctor's clinical freedom is another patient's delayed or forgone treatment — or perhaps pint of beer, no matter the financing mechanism. This is more apparent under a national health service, although it is there under all. How then do we reconcile the individual doctor's wish to do the best for his patient, the patient's wish for the doctor to do his best for him and society's wish for an efficient, equitable health care system? How do we embrace not just the individualistic ethics of virtue and duty but the social ethics of the common good?

First, it needs to be accepted that, by and large, medical ethical codes in concentrating on the individualistic ethics of virtue and duty are correct. Where they go wrong is in their misuse. Consequently, what we need in addition to a medical ethical code is a code of health care ethics. This has been suggested in principle by Weir, who points to the need for 'completing a set of ethics appropriate for health care as a whole', adding that this is 'likely to range wider than the ethics relating to individual professions and will inevitably reveal conflicts of interest and concern'.[8] True, but as Weir states, 'these differences can only be resolved by discussion of the underlying values and objectives of the interested groups'.

One, indeed perhaps the primary, advantage of having a code of health care ethics is that it will help to restrict the code of medical ethics to where it belongs: essentially in the world of the individual-doctor/individual-patient relationship.

But what would such a code look like? To establish that we need to be more clear as to what its purpose is. Essentially, this would be to try to protect the interests of the community of patients and potential patients (in other words, the aggregate society) in ensuring that good quality health care is available and accessible and that that proportion of society's resources devoted to health care is well used.

But why do we need such a code? The answer is very similar to the reasons given in Chapter 7 for why we need a medical ethical code. As individual citizens, our knowledge of health and health care in aggregate terms is poor; the search costs involved in finding out more and better are very high. Yet it concerns us that we have good quality care available to ourselves (remember Margolis' S-utility from Chapter 9?) and accessible to all (Margolis' 'fair share' notion). But we also want to know that 'our' resources devoted to health care are efficiently used, both in terms of X-efficiency and allocative efficiency. It is in everybody's interest that G', the perceived marginal productivity of the group's resources, is high. A health care ethical code can help to raise G'. Thus, such a code is first and foremost, as was the case for the medical ethical code, for reassurance. The difference is that the former is about reassurance for us as part of the aggregate community; in the latter it is reassurance for us as individuals *qua* individuals.

My proposed health care ethical code is as follows:

In order to ensure that good quality health care is available, all forms of health care which are ineffective should be abandoned.

Subject to legitimate concern about the costs involved in achieving it, the basis of health care should be equal access for equal need.

In order to protect society in the way in which its resources are used in health care, no policy should be pursued which could be pursued by an equally effective but less costly policy.

In order both to protect the citizenry's health and the use of their resources, priorities, planning and evaluation in health care should be subject to the principle that only those policies should be pursued which yield greater benefits than if the resources involved were devoted to some other end.

The values on which these decisions should be made ought to be those of society at large; where it proves difficult to elicit these directly, it may be necessary to rely on society's agents to provide the appropriate values. Given their involvement with individual patients, members of the caring professions might have to be excluded from acting as society's agents in these matters.

In other words, my code of health care ethics turns out to be quite simply the rational application of economic appraisal to health care.

Some interesting thoughts flow from this code. First, if politicians and administrators could refer to a health care code of ethics in their defence, it would strengthen their hand when faced with a shroud-waving clinician. Yes, they might say, *your* code says, 'Thou shalt not kill but need'st not strive, officiously to keep alive.' Ours says, 'Thou need'st not strive to keep alive, the few at the expense of the many', or again, 'Under my rights as a doctor, clinical freedom allows me to do whatever in my opinion is best for my patients.' To which the response is, 'Under my rights as a representative of the community, health freedom allows me to do whatever in my opinion is best for the community at large.'

Second, a code of practice of health service management would almost certainly flow from this health care ethical code, just as vast parts of medical practice are influenced by the medical ethical code. Thus, beyond the very early stages, health service management would become a profession built on its own ethical code. Such enhancement of the status of administrators and managers in health care is long overdue. A health care ethical code would help to serve this end.

Third, at a stroke, the use of economic appraisal in health care would become widely established. Within a very short space of time – given the pressure that there would be to conform to the health care ethical code – problems of output measurement, benefit valuation, incentive mechanisms, marginal costing, and so on, would be resolved or at least ameliorated.

Fourth, given the wording of the code, equity would become an *explicit* pillar of health care planning instead of, as it currently tends to be, everybody's loved but neglected aunt. Perhaps access is not the right dimension, yet it seems to combine the right degree of fair-sharing (*à la* Margolis), with recognition of the individual's right to choose (should he so wish) both his health care consumption and, insofar as the health service affects it, his level of health. To make health care consumption the goal of equity would not be acceptable in most Western democracies; it is too paternalistic. To make health the goal smells of, perhaps, romanticism – and certainly of monotechnicism.

There seems a lot to be said in favour of a health care ethical code.

10.5   Does economic appraisal work?[9]

While in principle the idea of introducing a health care ethical code based on the approach of economic appraisal is very appealing, can it be shown that it might work in practice? Can economic appraisal be made a practical reality?

The extent to which the approach is currently practised in health care is generally quite limited. Of course, much depends on how we define economic appraisal. The review by Drummond of over a hundred economic evaluative studies in health care[10] shows that the vast majority of these are at best based on cost-effectiveness analyses and consequently comfortably ignore the issue of benefit valuation. The introduction of 'option appraisal' for major capital schemes in the NHS has done much to promote economic appraisal more generally.

Of those studies which have attempted to measure benefit in monetary terms other than simply health service resource savings, the most frequently encountered approach is that from the human capital school. Less common is the approach of 'willingness to pay' on the part of the potential victim. This, as discussed in Chapter 4, is the more conventional (in economic terms, that is) demand-orientated method.

In other studies no overt, explicit attempt is made to measure benefit. In some of these it is *implied* that the costs are so great that the potential benefits could not possibly be of sufficient magnitude to justify them. (An example of this type of study is provided in the estimate by Neuhauser and Lewicki[11] of $47 million dollars as the marginal cost of detecting a case of colonic cancer in a protocol given approval by the American Cancer Society.) In others, the opposite is implied; that is, the costs are so small that the benefits are bound to be of a sufficient size to justify the project.

Yet again, a few studies have built on the decision rule of cost-benefit analysis regarding optimum levels of supply (namely, the equality of the ratios of marginal benefit to marginal cost in different programmes). Recourse has been had to this approach, albeit in a rather subjective manner, even in areas where measurement of output is particularly difficult as, for example, in studies of care of the elderly.[12]

In recent years cost-utility studies have come more to the fore. One which attracted particular attention, perhaps because it was the first of its kind to be published in the *British Medical Journal*, was the CUA of coronary artery bypass grafting by Williams.[13] One of the great advantages claimed for this form of appraisal is that it avoids the need to place money values on the outcomes.

In essence there are relatively few studies which justify being given the full status of cost-benefit analysis; some certainly, which are more correctly described as cost-effectiveness studies; two or three based on the implied-values approach; a few attempts to use the 'marginal analysis' framework of the cost-benefit approach; and a growing number based on the concepts of QALYs using cost-utility analysis.

It would be depressing even if perhaps understandable if we had to conclude that, given the complex and emotive nature of health and health care, decision-making on resource allocation in this sector was inevitably surrounded by less rationality and more prejudice than in any other activity of comparable magnitude. That may be the case; it is not inevitable. As McLachlan has indicated: 'One of the major policy requirements for most Western societies today is to eschew the drama for a while and examine critically with scientific techniques the dogmas and clichés with which the policy-making for medical care has been encumbered.'[14] It is suggested that cost-benefit analysis *can* help in this critical examination; but there is a danger that if we fail to understand the reasons why it has to date not been applied either widely or knowledgeably, then it may simply add to the existing dogmas and clichés mentioned by McLachlan.

In a perfect world with perfect information the idea of using economic appraisal to maximise the net benefit of health care to society, subject to some concern with equity is one to which most would subscribe. However, we do not live in a perfect world with perfect information. Consequently, many difficulties arise in attempting to apply the techniques of economic appraisal in health care.

First, while good data regarding health service costs are frequently available, this is less likely to be the case for those costs falling on patients and their relatives and friends.

Second, there is the question of the effectiveness of different types of care regime. Most (but not all) of the practices of medicine produce some improvement in the health state of the patient. Too often the extent of the improvement goes unquantified. These are problems which only the members of the medical and other health care professions can solve. It is not for the economist to say how effective various forms of care are. Yet it is unfortunate that the extent to which the medical profession is pressing for improvements in health status measurement (for example, through QALYs) is all too limited.

Third, as discussed in Chapter 4, the diffuse and frequently intangible outputs of the health care system − reduced mortality and morbidity and increased care and comfort − are often difficult to quantify. This is not surprising; essentially, what is sought is a means of measuring all possible health states and changes therein on some uni-dimensional measuring rod. It is difficult to see that we can achieve full-blown cost benefit analyses without it, although we can get a long way by simply applying the cost-benefit way of thinking. We need to watch here that perfection does not stop us adopting the good.

In essence the problems of output measurement stem from (1) the multi-dimensionality of health outputs and (2) the fact that the weightings, whether ordinal or cardinal, are inevitably value-laden. Thus, the *measurement* of health cannot be divorced from the *valuation* of health.

Clearly, and as has been demonstrated earlier in this book, there has been a lot of work in recent years in trying both to develop and to use Quality Adjusted Life Years in economic appraisal studies. If this work is successful − and some would argue that it is already sufficiently successful to be used in place of other existing output measures – then the problems of achieving multi-dimensional scaling of outcomes are solved, at least for health. But for some of the intangibles – such as anxiety – at present it is not clear that QALYs can cope as they are currently being developed. However, there may be ways of incorporating some of these intangible (and not strictly health) aspects into cost-utility studies in the longer run.

The problem of valuation arises partly at a methodological level, that is, how do we establish relevant values, but also, and as a prior issue, at the level of deciding on *whose* values to apply. This is one of the key questions facing any society in determining resource allocation in health care.

Certainly, this is not an issue that economists themselves can or indeed should attempt to resolve on their own; it involves a social or political judgment. Indeed, this view also incorporates an important *moral* judgment; that is, it ought not to be within the remit of the economist to exercise his preferences or value judgments for the various states of the world which he is asked to analyse. However, as Self, the arch-critic of cost-benefit analysis, has remarked, 'the difficulty with economic advice is that of disentangling predictions which are necessarily subject to wide errors from the values assigned to various outcomes', and he goes on to suggest that in a subtle way economists' own normative beliefs or theories are likely to affect the judgments about such values. [15] Consequently, despite the moral judgment expressed, it may well be that the economist cannot free himself from this subtle trap.

A fourth difficulty for the analyst is in trying to influence the processes of resource allocation through the application of economic appraisal. In the NHS, and it is true of all health services, the nature of decision-making is diffuse. This would seem to stem from the fact that in health care, perhaps to a greater extent than in any other 'industry', some of the most powerful workers and most influential decision-makers on resource allocation are, as it were, 'on the shop floor'; that is, the doctors. This results in the chain of decision-making frequently being lengthy and tortuous and embracing the value judgments of many different individuals. (And when it is 'illegitimately' short-circuited the problems may be even greater.) An understanding of these administrative, decision-making processes would seem to be a prerequisite for the economist wishing not only to apply economic appraisal to the health care sector but also hoping to influence health care resource allocation.

That understanding has not always been present, at least not in abundance, in the past.

This brief review perhaps goes some way towards explaining why comparatively few economic appraisal studies have been successfully conducted in health care. Does the rather pessimistic note mean that we should abandon the pursuit of economic appraisal in health care and with it our health care ethical code?

Certainly not; the fact that there are problems in practice in essence means two things. First, in attempting to apply economic appraisal techniques we need to be sure that the *level* of appraisal is appropriate. Second, there is still scope for developing and refining the methodology of economic appraisal in the health sectors, perhaps particularly in the form of cost-utility analysis.

Let us consider these two issues. First, there is a need to conduct an appraisal of the appraisal itself. We need, for example, to ensure that the *objectives* of the appraisal are correct. Again, it may be that identifying the costs and enumerating the effects (as opposed to quantifying and valuing the benefits) may on occasion suffice. In the Neuhauser and Lewicki example, quoted earlier, once they had calculated for a particular screening programme that the cost of detecting a case of colonic cancer was $47 million, it was scarcely necessary for them to value explicitly the benefits of such detection.

Yet again, identifying a series of 'implied values' – that is, the marginal costs in different programmes – for similar types of output (e.g. lives saved) will allow decision-makers to become more consistent in their decision-making and at the same time more efficient. (Thus, if the marginal cost of life saving in one field is £1 million and in another for saving similar lives £100,000, a switch of some resources from the former to the latter will increase the total of lives saved.) Indeed, as discussed in Chapter 4, it may be possible to take this implied-values approach still further and compare dissimilar outputs. Thus, while a greater degree of subjective judgment on the part of the decision-maker would then be required, none the less being forced to make explicit the weights he attaches to different outputs is likely to create a more efficient decision-making process. Indeed, there are considerable virtues in pursuing these 'implied values' more systematically and comprehensively and thereafter attempting to generalise from them to allow much more monetary valuation on the benefit side of existing cost-effectiveness studies, which, because of this lack, are in essence frustrated cost-benefit analyses.

It seems, therefore, that considerable advances can be made using the *approach* of economic appraisal, without necessarily having to solve all the difficulties above. The main reason for this is that with or without the explicit framework and approach of economic appraisal decisions will be made about resource allocation in health care. The fact that cost-benefit analysis cannot at present always be applied to health care problems, as the purists might wish, does not mean that it cannot be an important decision-aiding tool.

Second, there can be little doubt that there remains scope for improving upon the methodology of economic appraisal in the health care sector. Much has been done, for example see Drummond *et al.* Attempting to place monetary values on human life has become almost respectable. Measurement of health has become a major interdisciplinary industry with economists throwing in their lot with psychologists, operations researchers, sociologists and many others. The nature of health care production functions is being researched more and more. There is scope for further work; but the current level of activity suggests that some economists, at least, believe that some of these methodological problems are soluble.

Perhaps the best hope for getting an acceptable methodology for economic appraisal in health care rests with cost-utility analysis, and certainly this has advantages over both cost effectiveness analysis and cost-benefit analysis. With regard to the former, it is restricted to considering only one form of output while cost-utility analysis can potentially cope with several dimensions of ill-health (including death). Cost-benefit analysis requires ideally that all outputs be measured in money terms, whereas cost-utility analysis can stop short of this provided that the relevant outcomes can be contained in QALYs.

It is in large part this last proviso that is potentially a problem. QALYs include only health. If there is anything else that patients want from their treatment and care, then it is not in QALYs. However, the second problem is that cost-utility analysis only works if the opportunity cost of the resources included in the cost per QALY analysis is purely in terms of health or, if you like, QALYs. This immediately means that at best we are restricted to questions of health service resource use since other social service resource use and patient and patients' relatives' resources, such as their time, clearly have opportunity costs that embrace much more than just health. Thus cost-utility analysis at this level cannot get beyond addressing the question (but it is a rather important one!) 'How best can we maximise the QALYs from the health service budget?' These comments do not then mean that we have to abandon cost-utility analysis. Rather, there is a need for care in recognising not just the advantages of CUA over CEA and CBA but also the limitations of the approach embedded in CUA. The importance of these limitations will of course depend on how CUA is used and what questions it is asked to address. It does suggest again, however, that the use of CUA to try to assess the most efficient treatment for dealing with a specific health condition is less prob- lematical than its use on allocative efficiency questions across health care services more generally.

Perhaps economists have generally been guilty of overselling economic appraisal. A wider recognition of the problems of apply- ing the approach in health care can do nothing but good. It will help to silence the critics, or at least shift the focus of their criticism to more constructive targets. It may also reduce the current ten- dency for some non-economists to believe that the application of economic appraisal is a simple task. At the same time it will remind the economist that the tools of economic appraisal are somewhat blunt, in need of sharpening and, in the meantime, cannot be expected to carve out anything other than fairly crude – but none the less useful – appraisal apparatus.

What is very clear, however, is that there are insufficient incen- tives at present to promote efficiency and hence the use of economic appraisal in health care. The very existence of a health care ethical code should help. But other incentives are needed. It is to that issue that the next section is devoted.

10.6 Financing, budgeting[16] and remuneration

I do not want to pursue the general question of financing, although it must be clear that my own preferences lie at the collectivist end of the possible spectrum of financing mechanisms. Those, like myself, who place substantial weight on the equity goals of health care, are likely to share such preferences. (For a review of financing coming to this same conclusion see Donaldson and Gerard.[17]) Certainly, given a concern for equity, I can see little evidence to support charges, cost sharing or whatever we want to call it. (Nor can others; see for example Barer, Evans and Stoddart,[18] and Maynard.[19]) I can see situations where patients should receive money payments, for example, to reduce the transport and travel costs they might otherwise have to bear. (We might even pay them for their waiting time − just think of the impact of this if it came out of the clinician's budget!) Or again, as in France with ante-natal care, money payments might be used to induce attendance, particularly for preventive services. And there seems little reason to oppose payments to family or neighbour carers, especially where this can be shown to be more cost-effective than professional care.

On financing overall, given the importance that societies currently place not just on health care but on the level of spending on health care, in democratic countries there does seem to be a strong argument for having the decision on this lying with the government as the elected representatives of the people. This is clearly not the only way to attempt to control health care spending; it is certainly the most direct, seemingly the most democratic − and potentially the most successful.

Where the key to efficient resource allocation may well lie is in budgeting and in how we pay our doctors. The basic principle on which budgets should be built is that of competence in judging opportunity cost. By this I mean that a group of surgeons, with others working in the surgical arena and perhaps some lay representatives, are competent to determine such matters as the proportion of the total surgery budget which should go to neurosurgery and whether all the forecast extra monies next year should be devoted to ENT. An ENT surgeon is not competent to judge whether his call for additional resources should take priority over those of the geriatrician, the community nurse or the physiotherapist.

Frequently, budgeting is seen primarily as a mechanism of control. It is this; but it ought to be seen as fundamental both to rational planning and to economically efficient production functions. The former point is simply made: a structure of budgets along the lines of Table 10.1 will allow each level of competent decision-makers to plan priorities at their level of awareness.

Budgets would apply at the four different levels: for example,

Table 10.1 Budget structure

Level 1	Total budget
Level 2	Programme budgets (e.g. care of the elderly)
Level 3	Specialty budgets (e.g. dermatology)
Level 4	Clinical team budget (e.g. the clinical team of Mr Smith, the neurosurgeon)

for total health care; for programmes such as the elderly, the mentally ill or surgery; for a sub-programme or specialty such as neurosurgery; and for teams within sub-programmes (such as Mr Smith's clinical team in neurosurgery). Those responsible for the total health care of the region or area (politicians and/or the local health board/authority) would decide on the allocation to each programme. Programme Management Teams would then decide how to allocate their budget across their sub-programmes (e.g. the Surgical Management Team would split the surgery budget across the surgical specialties). Specialty Management Teams would then allocate their budget to clinical teams within their specialty. In this way priorities are set and, to a considerable extent, controlled through the budgeting process – at least insofar as resource allocation can be used as a mechanism for pursuing priorities.

At least as important but often less well understood is the role of budgeting in promoting economic efficiency. Left to his own devices and with little or no knowledge of the resources he is consuming, and certainly not of the price attached to them, the individual clinician may well get it right in terms of using the most effective treatments available for those patients he is able to treat. He will, however, almost certainly fall down on economic efficiency, both at the level of minimising resource use for a given output and maximising benefit from the resources available. If he doesn't know his resource use, how can he minimise it? If he has little control over what types of resources are available to him (i.e. he cannot substitute nurses for drugs and dressings), then he has no incentive to find out what mix of resources can best serve his patients' interests within some global level of expenditure. Give him a budget and the responsibility to manage it and the position will change. Whether these advantages of budgeting in principle will work in practice is heavily dependent on getting clinicians both to agree to operate the system *and* to work out, preferably among themselves, how best to deal with non-compliers. The best mechanism would seem to be to reward those who cooperate (let them have their pet machine) or let Mr Jones deal with the fact that his fellow neurosurgeon's overspending is directly affecting the resources available to Mr Jones' patients. This form of peer review with tightly controlled budgets so that Dr Paul's robbing Dr Peter's patients is there for Dr Peter to see (i.e. opportunity cost is made very visible to the right people) is to be encouraged. Essentially, it means, within surgery, for example, setting the surgeons at each other's throats. It is peer review that might work since non-compliance hurts and failure to deal with non-compliance in others hurts more.

It is this visibility of opportunity cost, both within a programme and across into adjoining programmes, that separates budgeting from the issues of cost information. It is the reason why budgeting may work, whereas disseminating cost information alone has seemed inadequate in changing behaviour regarding resource use.

One problem is how to set the budgets in the initial period. One way is to start with last year's spending − but to announce that during the year before you start the process means that everyone will attempt to increase their current spending. Ideally, but it may take time, the budgets should be determined by good medical prac-tice, which in turn should be based on economic appraisal. As a short run measure it would seem appropriate in the first year to adopt national average standards (i.e. to allocate out resources on the basis of what the average treatment of, say, a varicose vein operation consists of), or perhaps something just a little below that sum in order to have a contingency fund available to deal with the particularly deserving cases that will inevitably arise in the first year.

Certainly, such budgeting is very desirable if a code of health care ethics is to be translated into a practical management instru-ment. It is difficult to see otherwise how it will be possible to exercise the necessary control over the clinical freedom fighters.

Beyond the question of budgeting, however, lies the issue of more direct incentives through how we pay our doctors. There is now substantial evidence to show that the way that doctors behave is in part a function of how they are paid. (For examples, see Kras-nick et al.,[20] Rice,[21] and Rice and Labelle.[22]) This is not something that we should lament. Paying doctors for carrying out a particular activity means, *ceteris paribus*, that the probability that they will do it is thereby increased. Paying them still more is likely to increase the probability still more (although the evidence on this latter point is less strong).

Some have argued against fee-for-service medicine (see, for example, Culyer.[23]) But as a principle, I can see little wrong with it. The basic argument that is used against it seems to be that it will lead to 'overservicing'. It might, but that would seem to depend on two considerations. First, how high are the fees? And second, what is the optimal level of servicing?

If doctors are paid very low fees for some activities, they are unlikely to have any great incentive to carry them out. What a fee schedule could do, if properly constructed, is to encourage some activities and discourage others while, if so wished, the total level of activity of the doctor is held more or less constant. Indeed, one of the advantages of fees is that they can provide differential incentives to help to persuade doctors to pursue some activities more than others.

This is in no sense meant to imply that doctors are then doing something which is ethically or morally 'wrong' in taking account of the relative remuneration in using their time in different ways. Nor is it implying that doctors are 'just in it for the money'. I certainly don't believe that; I am simply suggesting that, given a higher reward for a particular activity, *ceteris paribus*, there is some higher probability that that activity will be conducted. (Of course there are other ways of trying to provide incentives than just fee-for-service medicine, as with the GP contract in the UK where remuneration is partly dependent on fulfilling certain targets – especially with respect to some preventive services.)

Second, there is a need to think through what is optimal care in various circumstances. This is where medical audit and clinical budgeting or resource management ought to marry up but seem not to. Best medical practice is efficient medical practice. What we want is some system of incentives to get doctors to practise this optimal level and type of care. But then we have first got to determine what the optimum is! This to me is the key to the promotion of efficient health care. Given the nature of the commodity health care as discussed in Chapter 3 and the agency relationship (see Chapter 6), the emphasis in health care policy-making on the achievement of efficiency has to be on the medical doctor and not on the patient. The normal 'rules' of demand do not obtain or are at best muted in the health care market. It is to the supply side and especially to the doctors that we have to look for the pursuit of efficiency. However as this does not come naturally to them, they need encouragement; they need sticks and carrots. While finance is only one form of incentive, it can be an important one. There is a need for more experimentation on how best to pay our doctors.

10.7   Will the NHS reforms get us there?

In this chapter I have tried to indicate some of the ways in which health care might be delivered more efficiently, and earlier I pointed additionally to the importance of equity in health care. Will the reformed NHS perform better? Will it encourage greater X-efficiency? In other words, will it get us to objectives just as well but at less cost? Will it promote allocative efficiency – will society's priorities for health and for health care be better structured and thereafter pursued? Can we expect that the equity goals of the NHS will be more adequately pursued?

Here I will not attempt a comprehensive review. (For a more detailed evaluation see Culyer *et al.*[24]) At the time of writing (June 1991) the NHS is very much in a state of flux and it is very difficult to judge how several parts of the reforms will settle down in practice. And by the time these comments are read much may have changed. Consequently, here I will pick on just certain aspects which appear to be particularly relevant to what has already been said in this chapter about promising ways of promoting these twin goals of any health service – efficiency and equity.

Two of the key issues in the NHS reforms which I want to examine are:

1.   Increased competition, embracing the idea of contracting and thereby introducing more of a separation between provision and financing.
2.   Consumer choice and agency.

As we saw in Chapter 2, there is a belief among economists that Adam Smith's invisible hand in the market-place can promote efficiency at the level of getting both social objectives met at least cost and also the most highly valued social objectives pursued. But the conditions for such successful pursuit of efficiency through competitive forces are quite (some would say very) severe. In the context of health care, the two most important are that consumers are well informed and that there are lots of firms in the market which are genuinely competing with one another.

Now there are relatively few areas of the economy where all the conditions which markets require to be efficient are in fact met. There is a danger in being too purist when we look at health care markets. But there does seem some very great distance between a market with well-informed consumers and many competing suppliers and the health care market. Here consumers are dependent to a large extent on the suppliers (especially the doctor agents) to help them to make rational decisions about optimal consumption in terms of both type and quantity of health care. Since the consumers cannot judge quality (at least insofar as that word embraces the impact of health care consumption on health status), they have to assume that the quality of care is adequate (as supported through the code of medical ethics). Furthermore, patients normally have to assume that all doctors are practising equally (high) quality medicine.

The evidence on medical practice variations as discussed earlier in the book does not lead one to be optimistic about the idea of equality of quality. Further, talking to medical colleagues, it is clear that they believe that some of their peers are better than others and, for example, would prefer certain surgeons to perform operations on them and to avoid other surgeons. (One could wish that this information were made more available to a broader group of potential patients; one wonders why in fact it is not.)

However, in the context of the NHS reforms will the idea of contracting for services lead to better, in the sense of more efficient, patient care? The evidence on competition is not too hopeful. However, most of this is drawn from experiences in the United States. There are in essence at least two problems in using this evidence to reach any conclusions for the NHS reforms. First, the nature of the competition in the US is very different from that in the NHS reforms and just because it doesn't seem to work well in the US does not mean necessarily that it will not work well elsewhere. Second, the US is a rather different type of society to the UK and the way that economists view issues tends also to be different. There is more often in the US a belief in competition per se; that competitive markets are 'a good thing'. (For a review of the

US evidence on competition in health care, see Culyer and Posnett. [25])

This attitude is reflected in Evans' [26] comments on the dangers of assuming that competition in itself is a good thing and in turn that price rationing (PR) is automatically to be preferred over non-price rationing (NPR).

> The superiority of PR ... rests on its conformity with a priori ethical principles defined over allocation processes, whatever results these achieve must be the best available, and actual outcome data are irrelevant ... If one accepts the faith, then PR is always to be preferred to NPR, and further discussion is pointless.

Certainly I would want the discussion to continue! Enthoven, [27] who was the person most responsible for the idea of the internal market, has written: 'When all of the alternatives have been considered, it becomes apparent that there is nothing like a competitive market to motivate quality and economy of service.' Unfortunately, and rather importantly, in the context of health care, the evidence that exists to support this statement seems at best limited.

It is not clear from the US evidence that competition in health care has served to keep costs down. Some studies, however, do suggest that vigorous competition can result in lower costs. (See, for example, Zwanziger and Melnick, [28] and Robinson and Luft. [29]) The lack of strength of the arguments on cost reduction is worrying because this is the area where we would have had most confidence that there might be some success. Not that the evidence is not there; it is simply that it is much less persuasive than we would have expected.

It is on the other side of the efficiency equation that observers seem to be more concerned. What will happen to quality? Here the evidence is very mixed and capable of very different interpretations. At the time of writing this would seem best summed up as: 'We don't know what the outcome is likely to be in terms of patient care but since this is less easily measured (despite the many attempts to do so in the US) and consequently less visible, then competition is much more likely to occur with respect to cost than quality.'

This is probably the central issue in the reforms. Will they lead to better patient care? Before this can happen, one would need to be convinced that health authorities who are purchasing services would be in a position both to describe what they want in their contracts in terms of quality and be able to monitor whether what they have purchased lives up to what they sought.

From the largely anecdotal evidence available at the time of writing it seems most unlikely that they will be able to do this. Health authorities are not currently well placed even to stipulate quality in contracts; they are even less well placed to monitor it. The concentration of thought and effort in contracting at present lies much more in assessing needs than in determining what the quality of the service is or ought to be and whether the contracts are fulfilled in terms of quality.

This is not surprising. It would be reasonable to respond to these comments by suggesting that the question of quality would be a problem and indeed is a problem in any health care system. That is agreed. The question is then: are the NHS reforms the way to go with respect to their reliance on increased competition through contracting?

Can we agree with van de Ven[30] when in the context of regulated competition in the Netherlands he writes: 'a strong argument for the expectation of good quality of medical care in a competitive health care system is competition itself. If the consumer is not satisfied, then he will choose some other provider or provider organisation.'

Whatever the evidence and the interpretation of it, all observers would seem to agree that the question of quality is a central issue. No one is against quality! But what is meant by it? Presumably it relates to patient benefit. Higher quality care is care that provides a greater benefit to the patients. And while health status improvement may well not be the only aspect of benefit in which the patient is interested, we can be confident that it is an important one.

Yet while all are agreed on this, the question of medical audit remains problematical. Since the issue of the effect on quality of care, or more precisely benefits to patients, is central to the whole exercise of the contracting business in the NHS reforms, let us look a little closer at the proposals here.

Working Paper 6[31] indicates that medical audit is 'the systematic, critical analysis of the quality of medical care, including the procedures used for the diagnosis and treatment, the use of resources, and the resulting outcome and quality of life for the patient'. Further, that paper states: 'The Government's approach is based firmly on the principle that the quality of medical work can only be reviewed by a doctor's peers.' And again: 'While the practice of medical audit is essentially a professional matter, management too has significant responsibility for seeing that resources are used in the most effective way, and will therefore need to ensure that an effective system of medical audit is in place.'

These comments from the working paper are worrying from the perspective of the central role of quality in the reforms. They assume that medical audit is the business only of medical doctors – except that the managers have some responsibility to ensure that the doctors do it. The implication is that in other respects medical audit is not the concern of managers. Indeed they imply that everyone bar the doctors should keep out. Yet if one looks at the way in which medical practice is currently evaluated today, in clinical trials for example, the extent to which the outcome measures adopted genuinely reflect what patients want from their treatment is rather limited. The profession, for example, has not been in the van in developing measures for health status. Indeed, it remains the case today that very often the effectiveness of cancer therapies is still presented in terms of the percentage survival after, say, five years (which tells us nothing about quality of life nor about what would happen to the patient otherwise).

Further, the evidence on practice variations has existed for a very long time, evidence which clearly shows that doctors are doing very different things when faced with essentially the same patients. Not all of the doctors can possibly be 'right' since the majority are doing something different from 'best practice', wherever that is on the spectrum. Yet this situation has been accepted by the profession for many years now. Why should we believe that the profession on its own, even with a push from the government, will now put its house in order?

And even if medical audit does produce some good results, on what criteria will it be based? It is not clear. What is clear is that if we leave it so much to the doctors they will not base it on any recognisable concept of efficiency.

And if they do come up with proposals that to be implemented will require change, will the members of the profession change? They might, but there are few grounds for optimism that they will do so unless the incentive structure is in place to get this to happen. The NHS reforms may help in this respect.

It is possible to argue that these sorts of problem exist in any organisation of health care. The question then is whether under the reformed NHS things will be better than under the unreformed NHS, and secondly whether these particular reforms could be improved upon. Within the terms of the competitive environment it is likely that there will be pressures to improve efficiency which may well lead to a lowering of costs in those parts of the country where the presence of a number of hospitals could lead to some element of genuine competition. This is unlikely to be the case in many parts of the country, however, and the US evidence, insofar as it is relevant, suggests that competition has to be quite vigorous before it can lead to any cost savings or at least to any that are sufficiently large to be picked up in any measurement attempts.

On quality there has been a missed opportunity to get medical audit and efficiency tied together. That is at best a pity because I would judge that it is this central issue that will decide in the end the success or failure of the reforms.

The issue of tying medical audit to efficiency could be tackled under any organisation of financing and delivery of health care. It could be that the internal market will provide a better structure of incentives than hitherto to get the doctors to change. This would seem a possibility, again not strictly because of the details of the changes but rather because the NHS is now 'on the move' as a result of the reforms, even if few (and I include myself in the majority here!) seem very clear where it is going and even fewer where it will end up. (For more discussion of the issues surrounding medical audit, see McGuire *et al.*[32])

In contracting per se, health authorities have been charged with assessing the needs of the population they are to serve. Unfortunately, partly because of the way that this has come from the health departments and partly because of the interpretation by health authorities and especially public health specialists, there is a danger of getting heavily involved in total needs assessments. Given some of the discussion in Chapter 6 on need, this pressure for assessing total need has to be resisted as strongly as possible. To attempt to assess total needs will be a very time-consuming exercise with little to be obtained from it that is ultimately valuable.

Total need is not a useful concept. It is difficult to understand what it means, and even if it did have some meaningful content as a concept, then it is not clear how one might begin to use it in the contracting process. Since 'total need', if it were to exist, would be too expensive to meet in full, then having measured it what would we do to decide what needs to contract for and what needs not to contract for? Presumably we would then ask: what needs can be met that yield the highest patient benefit per pound spent? That seems a reasonable question to pose. But the crucial point here is that this gets us into questions of marginal benefits and marginal costs, which is where the process should start.

In other words, we want to know what the marginal needs are that we are just failing to meet at present. Or, alternatively, at whatever level of spending and service we are operating, what is the next best buy in terms of the costs and benefits of expanding services? Or, if we take some resources from programme X, what benefits do we lose, and if we were to use these resources in programmes B or C, what benefits would we thereby obtain? Are the resources better spent on A, B or C? The answer to that question is very relevant to the contracting process. The point is that it at no stage requires that total needs are assessed; only marginal needs established in terms of marginal costs and marginal benefits.

On the question of consumer choice, which is, at least in the language of the reforms, a separate or additional component to that of competition, this is where I have to have real doubts about what is happening. There is already some limited evidence that there is less choice for patients in terms of which hospitals they are treated in as a result of the contracting process.

The key issue here, however, is not whether there will be more choice or not for patients. It needs to be stressed that this is in many ways one of the strongest ideological concepts lying behind the reforms. The more fundamental points are, first, do patients and citizens want more choice? And second, would such increased choice be an improvement in terms of efficiency and equity?

There has to be some doubt about whether patients want more choice. Certainly the government which introduced the reforms believed in the supremacy of patient choice. It is very much in line with the philosophy of 'consumerism' which is increasingly prevalent in British society more generally. But have the patients been asked whether they want greater freedom of choice? Or are we thrown back on to Bob Evans' criticisms of the PR and NPR debate, as raised above, that choice and freedom of choice are in themselves a good thing?

On the question of whether increased choice would lead to greater efficiency and equity, this would seem unlikely. There can be stress and regret involved in making decisions and many patients, lacking information – as we discussed in Chapter 3 – may well prefer to pass difficult decisions to the doctor. Thus patient utility may fall as a result of having to make choices.

Additionally it is not at all clear that more effective or efficient choices will emerge if patients have greater choice. The whole concept of agency in health care is predicated on the notion that patients are not well placed to make rational and informed choices. And the prospects for equity, at least across social classes, would seem likely to be diminished in any system where the benefits received become a function of individual choice.

It is in essence because of my strong attachment to the ideas surrounding the nature of the commodity health care as discussed in Chapter 3 and the concept of agency outlined in Chapter 5 that I have such great reservations about consumer choice leading to a more efficient health care system. Moreover, consumer choice does not fit well with the Margolis model on equity as spelled out in Chapter 9.

However, when we move beyond consumer choice per se and look at the reforms from the perspective of the agency relationship, then it is here that the position would seem to be much better, specifically with respect to the idea of the increased role of the GP as the agent for the patient through general practitioner budgets. While GP budgets are not normally couched in terms of the agency relationship, they seem to me to be designed to perform the role of encouraging a better agency role for the GP on behalf of his or her patients. In the context of a system-wide, as opposed to an individual-doctor individual-patient agency, role, I see the patient–GP relationship as central. If the patient cannot rationally decide about optimal consumption, the person in the system who is best placed to act as the patient's agent is the GP.

There are potential problems with the idea of GP budgets as built into the reforms, but at least they extend the role of the GP as the patient's agent. That seems to me a very important aspect of the reforms and a very welcome one. Certainly there is a need for care in how the process works in practice: how the budgets get set and how the GP makes the choices; how the high risk or high cost cases get their care catered for; how 'cream skimming' is avoided, etc. But the idea of giving GPs budgets within which they have to act as the patients' agents in maximising their patients' benefits is in principle one of the most attractive aspects of the reforms. (Other economists seem more cautious, however, in their attitudes to GP budgets. See, for example, Brazier *et al.*[33])

So the issue of patient choice in the reforms may be something of a red herring. What may be far more important is that within the reforms there is a better possibility of extending the role of the agency relationship, especially through the idea of GP budgets. Of course where one stands ideologically will affect one's judgment about the rights and wrongs of consumer sovereignty in health care and the broader concept of autonomy. (The former involves consumers, here patients, making the consumption choices; the latter assumes that the patients have the choice over whether or not to make the consumption choices.) I tend to favour the idea of patient autonomy, which then leads me to support the idea of GP budgets as a way of promoting a more complete agency relationship.

It has not been the intent to mount a full critique of the NHS reforms but rather to try to set certain aspects of the reforms into the context of this book. How other aspects will work out in practice will be clearer by the time this book is being read.

What might serve as an interim overall judgment on the reforms is that they are based on the premise that increased competition in health care is a good thing. That may be true. What is far less clear is whether there might not be better ways of proceeding. It is here that I would have to express my greatest doubts, i.e. with respect to the philosophy underlying the reforms. There certainly was a need to alter the structure of incentives in the old NHS, especially those operating in hospitals but also on doctors more generally. There is a need to get doctors to make decisions on the basis of efficiency criteria. The reforms may push them in that direction but there have to be serious doubts about that.

What would have been preferable would have been to adopt a less ideological stance and have asked the two central questions 'what do we want from our health service?' and 'how can we get the right set of incentives on the key players to get them to deliver?' The reforms are very quiet about the first point and they are suspect on the second. But we will have to wait and see whether through time they do deliver what the British want from their health service.

As a footnote to the discussion here (and not intended as a political comment), it is interesting to look back at some of the debate surrounding the introduction of the NHS in 1948. There has been much heated comment surrounding the introduction of the current reforms. But in terms of venom and eloquence it gets nowhere near the level achieved when the doctors, or at least the BMA, opposed the formation of the NHS. Let me quote, largely in amusement, from Foot's[34] book on Nye Bevan, the architect of the NHS, the words of Dr Cockshut, one of the leading spokespersons for the BMA at that time: 'We shall become West Indian slaves, they had complete security – subject only to two disadvantages. They could not own property and they could not move from their plantations. That is what will happen to the medical profession.' And Dr Cockshut again: 'The [NHS] Bill can be written in two lines: "I hereby take powers to do what I like about the medical service of the country – [signed] Nye Bevan, fuehrer." ' Whatever our health service and however it gets reformed, it is very clear that people care about it!

10.8 A final thought

It is to be hoped that at least some of the ideas proposed in this book will be welcomed by the medical profession, especially those whose ears are already attuned to the notion of promoting in a just fashion the health of the community at large. Certainly, the ideas have more relevance to an NHS type system than a more market-orientated one, although some are common to most health care systems, and in any case with the NHS reforms there is some blurring of this distinction. That is inevitable since the key to success here is seen in a genuine pursuit of a social cost–social benefit approach to health care, framed in a new code of health care ethics. At present, from my perspective, that is more likely to be achieved through some form of public ownership and public financing.

Much of what I have written may be construed by some of the medical profession as doctor bashing. That is not its intent. For me the basic issue is clear. We have found the most cost-effective solution to making knowledge of health and health care available to society: we train doctors. Doctors then have enormous power to influence the nature of health care delivery *whatever* the nature of the organisation and its financing. Yet that — the nature of health care delivery, its priorities and its objectives — should be the province of society when it comes to decision-making. Doctors then need to be socially controlled. In this process, an increasingly necessary one, economics can help.

All too much to hope for? All too much to hope for from economics, and far too arrogantly ambitious for an economist to claim, under the all too swashbuckling title of 'Economics, Medicine and Health Care', that his discipline can achieve it. But try substituting 'common-sense' or 'rationality' for 'economics'; little more than that is claimed in this context. And what then ...?

Notes

1. The description of economics as 'the dismal science' is attributed to Thomas Carlisle in 'On the Nigger Question' in 1849.
2. G. McLachlan and A.K. Maynard, 'The public/private mix in health care: the emerging lessons' in *The Public/Private Mix for Health. The Relevance and Effects of Change*, eds G. McLachlan and A.K. Maynard (The Nuffield Provincial Hospitals Trust: London, 1982), p 556.
3. A.K. Maynard, 'The regulation of public and private health care markets', in *ibid.*, p 506.
4. I. Wickings, J.M. Coles, R. Flux and L. Howard, 'Review of clinical budgeting and costing experiments', *British Medical Journal*, 287 (1983), p 576.
5. J.R. Hampton, 'The end of clinical freedom', *British Medical Journal*, 287 (1983), p 1237.
6. T.F. Andersen, M. Madsen and A. Loft, 'Regional variations in the use of hysterectomy', *Ugeskrift for Loeger*, 36 (149), 1987, p 2415. (In Danish.)
7. R.G. Evans, 'The dog in the night-time: medical practice variations and health policy' in *The Challenges of Medical Practice Variations*, eds T.F. Andersen and G. Mooney (Macmillan: London, 1990), p 117.
8. R.D. Weir, 'Incentives and rationing in health care', Maurice Bloch Memorial Lecture (Mimeo, Department of Community Medicine, University of Aberdeen, 1984), p 23.
9. This section is partly based on a report on a workshop on economic appraisal, A. Ludbrook and G.H. Mooney, *Economic Appraisal in the NHS* (Northern Health Economics: Aberdeen, 1984).

10. M.F. Drummond, *Studies in Economic Appraisal in Health Care* (Oxford Medical Publications: Oxford, 1981).

11. D. Neuhauser and A.M. Lewicki, 'What do we gain from the sixth stool guaiac?', *New England Journal of Medicine*, 293 (1975).

12. See, for example, I.D. Fordyce, G.H. Mooney and E.M. Russell, 'Economic analysis in health care: an application to care of the elderly', *Health Bulletin*, 39 (1981).

13. A. Williams, 'Economics of coronary artery bypass grafting', *British Medical Journal*, 291 (1985), p 236.

14. G. McLachlan, 'From medical science to medical care', *The Lancet*, 7491 (1967), p 630.

15. P. Self, *Administrative Theories and Politics* (George Allen and Unwin: London, 1972), p 2113.

16. At the time of writing the review of the resource management initiative was not available.

17. C. Donaldson and K. Gerard, *The Visible Hand: The Economics of Health Care Financing* (Macmillan: London, 1992 in press).

18. M.L. Barer, R.G. Evans and G.L. Stoddart, *Controlling Health Care Costs to Patients: Snare or Delusion?* (Ontario Economic Council: Toronto, 1979).

19. Maynard, 'The regulation of public and private health care markets', in McLachlan and Maynard, eds, *op. cit.*

20. A. Krasnick *et al.*, 'Changing remuneration systems: effects on activity in general practice', *British Medical Journal*, 300 (1990), p 1698.

21. T. Rice, 'The impact of changing Medicare reimbursement rates on physician induced demand', *Medical Care*, 21 (1983), p 803.

22. T. Rice and R. Labelle, 'Do physicians induce demand for medical services?' *Journal of Health Policy, Politics and Law*, 14 (1989), pp 3, 587–600.

23. A.J. Culyer, 'Competition and markets in health care: what we know and what we don't', *NHS White Paper Occasional Paper No. 3* (Centre for Health Economics, University of York: York, 1989).

24. A.J. Culyer, A.K. Maynard and J. Posnett, eds, *Competition in Health Care: Reforming the NHS* (Macmillan: London, 1990).

25. A.J. Culyer and J. Posnett, 'Hospital behaviour and competition' in *ibid*.

26. R.G. Evans, 'Health care in Canada: patterns of funding and regulation' in McLachlan and Maynard eds., *op. cit.*

27. A.C. Enthoven, 'Reflections on the Management of the NHS', *Occasional Paper No. 5* (The Nuffield Provincial Hospitals Trust: London, 1985).

28. J. Zwanziger and G.A. Melnick, 'The effects of hospital competition and the Medicare PPS program on hospital cost behaviour in California', *Journal of Health Economics*, 7 (1988), p 301.

29. J. Robinson and H. Luft, 'Competition, regulation and hospital

costs 1982 to 1986', *Journal of the American Medical Association*, 257 (1988), p 267.

30. W.P.M.M. van de Ven, 'A future for competitive health care in the Netherlands', *NHS White Paper Occasional Paper Series No. 9* (Centre for Health Economics, University of York: York, 1988).
31. *NHS Review Working Paper No. 6, Medical Audit* (HMSO: London, 1989).
32. A.J. McGuire, P. Fenn and K. Mayhew, 'The economics of health care' in *Providing Health Care: The Economics of Alternative Systems of Finance and Delivery*, eds, McGuire, Fenn and Mayhew (Oxford University Press: Oxford, 1991).
33. J. Brazier, J. Hutton and R. Jeavons, 'Evaluating the reform of the NHS', in *Competition in Health Care: Reforming the NHS*, eds A.J. Culyer, A.K. Maynard and J.W. Posnett (Macmillan: London, 1990).
34. M. Foot, *Aneurin Bevan, 1945–1960* (Palladin: London, 1975).

Index